Everything is Practice

With gratitude

Metta,

gil

Everything is Practice

A GUIDE FOR INSIGHT MEDITATION RETREATS

GIL FRONSDAL

TRANQUIL BOOKS

Tranquil Books
108 Birch Street
Redwood City, CA 94062

ISBN 978-0-9845092-6-3

Contents

Preface

On Insight Meditation retreats, we set aside time to connect with ourselves more deeply and to see more clearly into our lives, experiencing for ourselves the transformative power of extended periods of meditation.

This inspiring guide for practicing on silent Insight Meditation retreats is deeply intertwined with Gil Fronsdal's vision for the Insight Retreat Center (IRC), which was established in 2011, a vision that is founded on the idea that the practice unfolds best in a field of generosity, gratitude, and goodwill. In realizing that vision, all IRC retreats are offered free of charge. The center is entirely sustained by the community of practitioners and volunteers who are inspired by the practice, teachings, and values found at the center.

The IRC community has grown significantly since the COVID-19 pandemic in 2020, when we began offering online retreats. Due to the enthusiastic response to these retreats, they have become a regular part of IRC's offerings. These virtual retreats have greatly expanded the range of people who can participate in retreats. We can now include those for whom travel to IRC may not be an option and those with physical limitations or home sibilities. We can now have many more participants than our residential retreat center can accommodate.

***

Each chapter of this practical guide touches on aspects of practicing on retreat. It is informed by Gil's fifty years of meditation practice and his decades of teaching and guiding countless practitioners. He wrote each chapter with the care and generosity at the heart of his teaching.

Gil navigates the entire arc of retreat practice—from the moment we sign up for a retreat to the many aspects of the retreat experience and finally to the integration period when we return to daily life activities. He points out that the retreat experience begins when we first sign up. He urges us to reflect on the attitudes we bring to preparing for the retreat and he encourages us to take the time to reflect on our more profound aspirations.

If we are new to silent meditation retreats, this book can guide us to be more at ease with an unfamiliar experience that may even seem daunting.

If we are experienced with these insight meditation retreats, the book can be invaluable in helping us expand our understanding of what it means to say, "Everything is practice." The moments we might spend in formal sitting or walking meditation are neither more nor less valuable than the presence we might bring to washing our hands or putting on our shoes.

Gil points to a mature practice that includes every aspect of ourselves, with nothing left out, fostering a deep sense of self-acceptance and understanding––a practice that both provides for the solitude of deep meditation and the connection of practicing in community with others. He emphasizes a practice that points to the freedom possible in every aspect of our lives, including in our wider world.

This guide clarifies that the meditation instructions we receive on a retreat, though they can be very significant, are only one aspect of the retreat. When practitioners sit retreats over the years, other aspects of being on retreat can become even more relevant. For instance, sometimes retreatants find humor as they realize they may have spent a week stressing and rushing in preparation for a week of not stressing and rushing. Even though these retreats are silent, the interpersonal aspects of sitting in community can come to the forefront, both the aspects we are attracted to and the things we are aversive to. At other times, a complicated relationship with meals might come into focus, or on the other hand, a heartfelt appreciation of all the beings that make our meals possible.

In the following pages, Gil guides us through the various stages of a retreat, bringing his clarity and wisdom to the challenges and rewards that may arise as we explore the landscape of our inner world.

I am deeply grateful to Gil for sharing his deep wisdom and compassionate guidance through this book. May his teachings serve as a guiding light, illuminating the path of Insight Retreats and inspiring us to engage with this profound journey wholeheartedly, bringing forth profound transformation and liberation.

With deep gratitude,
Ines Freedman

Introduction

While this book is a guide for insight meditation retreats, I often think the word return better expresses the benefits that come with these periods of meditation practice. Return more accurately conveys the way in which meditating in a contemplative setting can be a profound homecoming. Retreat, on the other hand, may suggest a withdrawal or a retreat from our ordinary life. Still, because it's the accepted convention, retreat is the word I use throughout this guide.

In much the same way that deep rest revives our vitality, sleep restores mental clarity, and healing brings us back to good health, meditation retreats return us to wonderful states free from stress, preoccupation, and exhaustion. In the silent environment of a retreat center, our mind, heart, and body can settle into health and harmony. While meditation states are sometimes called "altered states of consciousness," it's actually the fragmented, distracted, and emotionally challenged mind of daily life that is better understood as an unnecessarily altered state. In contrast, time spent on a meditation retreat can return us to a wholesome and natural mind. Our inner life in meditation may seem altered when it is rarely—if ever—experienced

1

elsewhere. Even so, when the mind is deeply settled, it gives us a taste of a natural mind, free of attachments and anxiety. Meditation retreats are training grounds for discovering and supporting our potential for a healthy heart and mind.

For the Buddha, mindfulness practice is a return to our "ancestral homeland," which is always available here and now. He defined this native land by the four foundations of mindfulness: body, feelings, mental states, and mental processes. By settling into our body, opening up to our feelings – especially the more profound ones – discovering healthy mind states, and becoming wise to how our mind works, we "return" to a territory we may have lost touch with but have never actually left.

Over time, it becomes clear that meditation and meditation retreats are a return to natural states of peace, happiness, love, and wisdom. The more we are caught up with attachments, aversions, anxiety, and conceit, the more we withdraw from feeling whole, free, and harmonious. Understanding how much is lost in this withdrawal reminds us how beneficial it is to "return" to our homeland.

While meditation retreats are wonderful places for this return, even more importantly, they are training grounds for learning how to remain at home in ourselves. Any degree of calm and settledness can highlight how we lose this calm. On retreats—and in meditation in general— rather than being disappointed by this loss, we bring mindfulness to clearly see how the loss happens. We learn the tricks of our distracting thoughts, the pull of our difficult emotions, and the persistence of our desires and aversions. The wiser we are about how these tricks operate in us, the easier it is to avoid their allure and promise. It is a wisdom that can show us what and how to let go of anything that doesn't support our inner health.

The more we can let go of the mind's tricks, the deeper we can settle into the wellsprings of well-being, stillness, and spiritual health. This, in turn, reveals even more profound, more subtle forms of attachments seldom seen in the busy mind of daily life. The repetition of this three-step pattern of meditative calm, seeing how the mind operates, and letting go can be a gentle, spiraling homecoming into our depths, the end of which is profound freedom.

The process, from the initial calming when we begin meditating to the most profound experience of freedom and independence, provides us with the understanding and tools for practicing mindfulness in daily life. It provides a reference for an alternative to a busy, scattered, and attached mind. If we return to this alternative, however partial the return may be, the practice we learn on retreat comes alive in the rest of our lives.

An invaluable aspect of participating in meditation retreats with other people is the benefit that comes from community practice. Meditation retreats can be challenging, especially for people new to the absence of social conversations and to the many meditation sessions throughout the day. The presence of others engaged in the same endeavor can encourage, even inspire, a dedication that lessens the sense of challenge and increases our commitment to practice.

Practicing with others on retreat also contributes to a deeper understanding of our reactions, judgments, desires, and fears in the presence of others. This, too, provides opportunities to become wise to the tricks of the mind and the vulnerabilities of the heart. We slowly learn what we can let go of and what we can strengthen to live wisely and kindly with others.

With mindfulness, we bring with us, wherever we go, a profound sense of being home in ourselves and so with anyone we are with. The freedom we discover through meditation is portable, so we can learn to be at ease and free anywhere. Wisdom teaches us to let go of the attachments that keep us separated from some people and attached to others.

Group meditation retreats are profound times to discover a non-separated, unattached sense of community. Meditating together in silence cuts through many of the usual projections, fears, and reactions we might easily have with others. Meditating together, we sense people's sincere dedication to being mindful of their life challenges and their spiritual wholeness. As a result, by the end of a seven-day retreat, people sometimes feel closer to other meditators than they would if they spent the week talking with them.

In this way, retreats are not just a return to inner health but also a return to social health – i.e., a healthy, perhaps more natural way of relating with others. What we learn about generosity, goodwill, care, and respect for others on retreat shows us how to be in life after the retreat. Retreats train us to find our way back to this healthy way of sharing our native homeland with all beings.

This retreat manual contains essays I wrote over many years to support those who attend retreats at the Insight Retreat Center in Santa Cruz, California. I also wrote them to express my love for mindfulness, meditation, and retreats. I hope this book inspires and supports you in undertaking these retreats. Please read the book slowly, perhaps no more than a chapter or two a day. Rather than filling yourself with information and ideas all at once, gradually reading the book might allow you to contemplate and practice what is written and so stay close to the simplicity that is a hallmark of mindfulness practice. A frequent saying in our tradition of Buddhism is, "If it is not simple, it is not Vipassana."

NOTE:

This book describes the terrain of meditation practice on a retreat. It does not provide a map of the path through this terrain. It is your task to discover and forge your own path home to a heart set free.

Everything is Practice

1

Retreat Practice

In the years before he attained liberation, the Buddha
devoted extended periods of time to meditation. After his
awakening, he continued meditating. Though his daily life
included both times for meditation and teaching, he would
periodically retreat into the forest for weeks and months of
meditation before returning to continue teaching and
guiding others in their practice.

Since then, many people have followed his example by
retreating to monasteries and wilderness settings. There
they have devoted themselves to mindfulness, concentration, loving-kindness, compassion, and, most importantly,
to attaining liberation. They have explored and healed
their hearts and minds. They have delved into profound
silence and peace from which great wisdom flows. And,
like the Buddha, they then returned to society to share the
benefits of their practice with others.

When Buddhist meditation was mainly the preroga-
tive of monastics, spending long periods in the wilderness
or monasteries was the primary means of engaging in
extended periods of meditation. Now that a growing number of lay people practice meditation, our modern world
has given birth to "meditation retreats" and "retreat cen-

ters," where people take time out from their daily lives to participate in a meditative life.

Meditation retreats are powerful and nurturing places for developing spiritual practice. With a daily schedule devoted to meditation, retreats foster a continuity of practice that lets the benefits of the meditation blossom. By protecting participants from their usual responsibilities and distractions, retreats allow for immersion in the practice. As a way of "retreating" from our daily lives and habits, retreats contribute to new perspectives and reflections to bring back to our daily lives.

In the Insight Meditation tradition, the typical retreat is 7 to 10 days long, though some are shorter and others longer. Most of the day is devoted to meditation, following a schedule that alternates between sitting and walking meditation. There is usually a rest period of an hour or so after each meal. The retreat teachers guide and support the retreatants with daily dharma talks and a morning session with meditation instructions. A few times throughout the retreat, participants meet with one of the teachers to discuss their practice.

Insight retreats are designed to create an environment of simplicity that sharply reduces the activities and concerns that typically distract us from the simple practice of meditation. For this purpose, retreatants spend most of their time in silence. That means, for instance, that retreats are phone- and Internet-free zones. While the lack of ordinary social conversation and external stimulus may feel alien at first, over time, nearly every retreatant I've met has come to value the silence and simplicity found on retreat. A settled, peaceful mind is hard to come by in our harried, always-connected modern lifestyle.

Even though all retreatants share the same pared-down schedule, their personal experiences vary considerably because of the different backgrounds, needs, intentions, and understandings they bring to the retreat. The practice matures differently in different people at different times and stages of their lives. In this sense, there are as many retreats going on as there are participants. On any given retreat, some people discover the immense beauty of a tranquil and liberated heart. Others find themselves face-to-face with unresolved personal issues. Others discover the benefits of slowly and systematically cultivating patience, mindfulness, or loving-kindness.

Based on my experience as both a practitioner and meditation teacher, I view the many functions of meditation retreats as falling into four general areas: recovering, discovering, cultivating, and freeing. Sometimes an individual's retreat experience focuses primarily on one of these. Other times, several or even all come into play. With each of these functions comes the possibility of great joy, peace, and insight.

Recovering

Retreats are a great place to recover and unwind from life's many stresses. For instance, people often come to retreat in a state of sleep deprivation, and for them, retreats provide a crucial opportunity to obtain deep rest, often much better than they get on a vacation. Retreats can promote much-needed relaxation for people who arrive carrying significant tension. For those who have been too busy or preoccupied to tend to their emotional lives, retreats are a safe place to let unresolved emotions surface and unfold. For example, retreats can be helpful for someone who's going through the grieving process after a significant loss. The many days of a retreat can also allow old, long-avoided emotions to finally come into awareness. Sometimes recovery and healing can only happen after shedding a backlog of tears.

Spending time on retreat can also help a person recover values, feelings, and insights that have been forgotten, neglected, or covered over by daily life. As the familiar concerns of making a living, caring for a family, or dealing with crises recede in the silence, time on retreat can help people remember intentions and priorities on which they want to base their lives.

Discovering

Retreats allow people to step out of their regular activities to discover what is really going on in their lives. Emotions, thoughts, intuitions, and unexamined issues can show themselves when we're no longer racing around and distracted by busyness. A retreat can be a chance for people to catch up on their lives. It can be a place to discover a greater capacity for well-being than we'd previously known.

Uninterrupted mindfulness greatly enhances the discovery process. Sustained attention and calm can help people see the underlying operating principles of how they live. Most people don't know why they do, say, or think what they do. It's common for someone on a retreat to discover with great surprise how much they have based their life on deeply held beliefs and attitudes they can no longer believe. While self-discoveries can be painful and challenging, they are essential if we are to begin to become free of them.

The sustained mindfulness cultivated on retreat can be likened to looking at our present experience through a microscope. This magnification allows us to see the universal characteristics of human life. This seeing can be more profound and more transformative than any insight we might have into our unique personal psychology.

While on retreat, we can also discover the benefits of being relaxed, letting go, and seeing clearly. We might uncover and question the belief that clinging tightly or being tense is helpful to ourselves or others. And we may come to appreciate that our hearts and minds function much better when they're at peace.

Cultivating

The mind is not a thing; instead, it consists of many mental processes influenced by the conditions that bear on them. The mental activities we engage in are the primary influences that shape which mental processes operate in us and how they do so. If we frequently worry, we are, in effect, training the mind to worry more. If we spend much of our mental activity wanting things or being angry, we strengthen desire and anger. If we emphasize goodwill, we cultivate more of it. And if we practice generosity and mindfulness, the capacity to be generous and mindful becomes stronger.

An essential part of Buddhist practice involves taking responsibility for the influences shaping our minds. If we don't take the initiative, our minds will be shaped by influences we may not want or even be aware of. One of the important ways of taking responsibility is cultivating those mental processes that bring out the most beneficial aspects of our humanity.

A retreat is an ideal place to cultivate the mind in this way. It provides the rare opportunity to devote much of the day to developing mindfulness, concentration, patience, equanimity, loving-kindness, and wisdom. We have time to repeatedly wake up to the present moment and reestablish attention.

As the mind is cultivated, it has a greater and greater capacity for being calm and at ease. Rather than being overwhelmed by life's difficulties, we have more inner balance, strength, and wisdom to respond in helpful ways to life's vicissitudes.

For most people, it's easier to experience deep states of stillness and peace or to be filled with pervasive feelings of loving-kindness or compassion when meditation is practiced with the consistency that's possible on retreats. Some of the most beautiful states of mind are available to minds that have been cultivated.

Freeing

In Buddhism, recovery, discovery, and cultivating the mind are not ends. They are essential steps in freeing the mind from its mental afflictions. The good news of Buddhism is that it's possible to free the mind from its contracted states. It's possible to let go of clinging and the limitations clinging creates.

While liberation can be experienced anytime and any-where, meditation retreats are one of the most fertile places for experiencing this freedom. Focusing ourselves fully on practicing meditation allows for the clear seeing and strength of mind that is needed before one can let go of clinging, fear, greed, and aversion. Retreats also provide support and safety that can make it easier to experience feelings of vulnerability that may come with the release of clinging. For people new to the practice, degrees of free-dom may come with learning to let go of preoccupations with people and things not at the retreat. For people who focus too much on themselves, freedom may be learning to let go of their preoccupation with themselves.

One of the wonderful things about meditation retreats is the way they bring out the best in people. One reason this happens is that mindfulness practice reduces reactivity in which unhealthy impulses may predominate. The attention to the present moment that meditators develop makes it easier to avoid participating in the mind's unwholesome forces. Instead, the spacious time and simplicity of retreats are conditions that bring forth and help sustain the most beautiful, wholesome states our minds are capable of. Retreats are places where people can grow in kindness, generosity, integrity, resilience, wisdom, and compassion.

All the benefits we experience on retreat are not generated for ourselves alone. As we return to society when the retreat is over, we naturally share these benefits with others. This way, meditation retreats are the spawning ground for a more significant, pervasive transformation. By recovering, discovering, cultivating, and freeing, we become a positive force that can change the world.

2

Preparing for a Retreat

Being well-prepared for a meditation retreat supports a good beginning once we arrive. It facilitates an easeful settling into the practice and a quicker immersion into the focused mindfulness of your direct experience. With adequate preparation, you can begin the retreat with fewer and less compelling preoccupations, which might otherwise take extended retreat time to quiet down.

Before discussing some ways to prepare for a retreat, I want to mention that being unprepared doesn't have to be a problem. The experience of being unprepared offers its own benefits. We can learn how to be present and equanimous with whatever resulting challenges arise. Being unprepared might provide an opportunity to better understand issues in our lives that contribute to being regularly unprepared. For example, why did we arrive exhausted? Are we carrying unresolved personal issues? Have we been too casual or complacent in coming to the retreat? Were we unclear about our intentions in participating?

From one perspective, being prepared and being unprepared are both good ways to start a retreat. They each offer opportunities for practice. Still, being prepared is generally more satisfying and can lead to settling into the retreat more quickly. Preparation can be external, such as arranging the circumstances of our lives to be in enough order that they don't intrude during the retreat. And it can be internal preparation that orients our mind to be ready for the retreat practice.

External Preparation

An unhurried life supports mindfulness practice. Your practice will be supported when you prepare for the retreat far enough in advance that you aren't rushed in packing and traveling. By preparing early you may be less liable to forget something important, as you might when packing at the last minute. You'll have the chance to review and confirm that you have everything you need. If retreat center websites or registration confirmations provide a list of things to bring, it's helpful to check the list. It is important to bring adequate medication(s) if needed, as it can be disruptive to fill a prescription while at the retreat center. It's also helpful to leave at home things you won't need. Leaving reading material behind is useful, so you're not tempted to read during the retreat.

An unhurried life is also supported by taking care of family, home tasks, or work responsibilities well before you leave. This can include having backup plans in place for any people you may have recruited to take on essential responsibilities, such as caring for family members and pets or covering important tasks and decisions at work. With a good backup plan in place, you can avoid being contacted during the retreat.

Most insight retreats are designed as full-immersion periods of practice with no phone, text, email, web, or mail contact with the outside world. Such external contact can stir us up with things to think about and emotions to process, hampering or disrupting the deepening of concentration. Therefore, part of preparing for a retreat is letting family, friends, and co-workers know you will be unavailable. To some people, you might explain the nature of a meditation retreat and why you will be unavailable, but to others, you might simply prefer to say you're taking a much-needed break in a place where you will be offline and unplugged.

Another part of retreat preparation is considering what you will do in the day or two after the retreat. Plan ahead so that you can have a gradual return to your everyday life.

If you are going to a retreat center for the first time, study the center's website to see if it provides any unexpected information that might be important. The website may have a FAQ section or post the typical retreat schedule.

Internal Preparation

One of the most useful preparations for retreats is getting adequate sleep beforehand. One reason to pack and otherwise get your affairs in order well before the retreat is so you don't have to stay up late doing these things the night before.

You can also prepare your body. Engaging in physical stretching, such as yoga, during the week or two before a retreat can make settling into the many hours of meditation easier. A posture that works well for one meditation session a day at home may need extra support for managing the frequent sitting periods at a retreat.

Some people find it helpful to begin meditating more often a week or two before the retreat. This can help you ease into the many hours of meditation you will be engaged in. If you don't have a daily meditation practice, beginning one a week or two before the retreat is particularly useful.

It's also helpful to spend time before a retreat considering your motivation. What purpose do you anticipate or hope the retreat will have for you? What motivated you to sign up? How well do you understand the usual instructions in mindfulness meditation? If not very well, listen to audio recordings of retreat instructions (available at

Audiodharma.org and Dharmaseed.org). Are you planning on following the instructions at the retreat, or do you have other plans for your practice? If the latter, let the teacher know at the start of the retreat.

While motivation and purpose are valuable, they can also lead to expectations, and expectations can lead to frustration. People often come to retreat with ideas or agendas for what should happen. They may have expectations about any number of things—the meditation experience they'll have, retreat life in general, fellow retreatants, or which personal issues they will address during the retreat. While imagining what might happen on a retreat is normal, expectations about what should happen quickly lead to disappointment and distract us from noticing what is happening in our direct experience. So in preparing for a retreat, it is highly recommended that you consider your expectations. You might also consider transforming these expectations into simple aspirations or possibilities you're open to without insisting on them or waiting for them to occur. Knowing your expectations and holding them lightly will make the vicissitudes of a retreat easier.

Before the retreat, consider if you have any significant unresolved issues that might need to be addressed during the retreat. If there are any, it can be beneficial to spend time contemplating them. This includes thinking of appropriate ways of putting them aside until after the retreat when you might have a new and better perspective. Letting the retreat teacher know about these issues might also be useful.

In important ways, a retreat begins when you first think about going. Filling out the application, being accepted, making plans to go, and traveling to the retreat are all part of the retreat itself. Your thoughts, aspirations, and preparations for the retreat are tilling the soil for something to sprout in the field of your retreat. If you prepare for a retreat with care and love for your Dharma practice, you will undoubtedly prepare a fertile ground where a lot of good will grow.

3

Meditation Instructions on Retreats

A central part of a meditation retreat is the ongoing meditation instruction the teachers provide. The instructions are treasures based on the cumulative meditation experience of many people, ultimately traced back to the meditation practice of the Buddha. They are taught as means to calm our agitation, understand our minds, heal our wounds, improve the quality of our inner life, and allow us to be the beneficiaries of liberating Insights. They are treasures that create inner wealth.

At the same time, none of the meditation instructions the teacher gives on retreat are the actual instructions given by the Buddha. The teachings of the Buddha that survive contain broad-stroke instructions, but they require clarification and added details. In addition, his instructions need to be applied and adapted to ever-new cultural settings and personal circumstances. In this way, meditation instructions are cultural constructs that provide important suggestions for exploration, experimentation, and evaluation of our meditation practice. The longer we practice with a particular meditation instruction, the more the meditation practice is modified to fit us better. It's somewhat like walking in new shoes: the more we walk, the more they gradually wear in and better conform to our feet.

There are many styles or techniques for Vipassana (Insight) meditation, each with very different instructions (discussed briefly in chapter 5). Regardless of the type of Vipassana instruction offered, however, one of its most important functions is to help us understand our minds. In a sense, the instructions are mirrors for us to notice what works and doesn't work in settling us into our meditation. For example, in attempting to follow some instructions, we can learn what makes it challenging to do so. We might learn about such tendencies as getting swept up in distracting thoughts or our resistance, doubt, expectations, perfectionism, impatience, or other attitudes. Learning about these tendencies provides an opportunity to become wise about them, both in terms of our attitudes toward them and ways of overcoming them.

Noticing how we practice with instructions is also a way to learn how to fine-tune the different faculties of mind involved in meditation. For example, we can learn how to find the ever-changing balance between effort and relaxation, focus and open receptivity, determination and allowing, mindfulness and concentration, and between an embodied sensing of present-moment experience versus a clear cognitive recognition of what is happening in the present.

When we are not successful at fulfilling the explicit or implicit purposes of any given meditation instruction—for instance, to become concentrated, calm, mindful, Insightful, or to experience some degree of letting go—the instruction is nevertheless successful if we have learned more about ourselves, and perhaps thereby become wiser about how to navigate our inner landscape. In this way, even "failing" with the instructions may mature us along the path of practice. Sometimes people discover more about inner freedom by "failing" meditation than by "succeeding."

Meditators have many purposes for doing meditation. Having a good understanding of purpose is useful because we can then adjust the instructions to better fit our purpose. Aiming to develop a kinder attitude in mindfulness may require a different approach than aiming to develop concentration. Being mindfulness of difficult emotions may be different than mindfulness that rests in the breathing. The skills needed to practice with distracting thoughts may be different than those for practicing with physical pain. While the ultimate purpose of meditation may be spiritual liberation, attending to more immediate purposes may be necessary first.

Regardless of our purpose for and approach to practicing mindfulness meditation, it is helpful to keep it simple.

The Indian Vipassana teacher Munindra-ji often said, "If it is not simple, it is not Vipassana." Learning to have clear, present-moment awareness that retains a simplicity of being is a skill learned through practice. When confronted with what initially appears to be complicated instructions, the task is to discover how to practice them in a simple, unhurried manner, maybe focusing on a particular aspect of the instruction.

In doing Insight meditation, it can be helpful to have available, in the back of the mind, a concise statement describing the essence of the instruction. This may help us stay close to the simple awareness practice at Vipassana's heart. One such statement is, "Be still and gaze upon everything kindly." Another might be, "Trust awareness." Or perhaps, with a loving and supportive attitude, "Stay."

During the early decades of teaching Vipassana in the West, the Western Insight teachers developed a somewhat standard set of instructions that are a "middle way" that works well as foundational instructions for a wide variety of people and a wide range of personal circumstances. They are the basis for realizing the full potential of Insight practice and a great support for doing other forms of meditation. These basic instructions sit in the middle of the many ways the instructions can be modified. One person may be instructed to do the practice with more effort while another may be told to apply less effort. One person may be advised to do the practice with acceptance of whatever is happening; another may receive the recommendation to be less accepting of distracting thoughts, to let go of them as soon as possible. Someone who is disconnected from their body may be instructed to focus on the body; someone with a lot of body awareness may benefit from greater attention to the mind. At different times in one individual's practice life, one or another of these modifications might be useful. On retreat, ideas for how to modify the instructions can be one of the topics for discussion in meetings with the teachers.

Generally, there are two forms of meditation instructions provided on retreats. The first is for seated meditation; the other is for walking meditation. Occasionally, eating instructions are also provided at the start of a retreat. The rest of this chapter focuses on instruction for seated meditation.

The standard Insight Meditation retreat instructions for seated meditation are given progressively over the retreat, with each morning's instruction building and expanding on the previous teachings. The entire set of instructions can be provided all at once, as they often were when I practiced with Ven. U Pandita Sayadaw in Burma. However, this is a lot to remember and can give the impression that the practice is complicated. Simple instruction on the first day often works well for settling into a retreat, as people sometimes arrive on a retreat with agitated minds. For this reason, instructions on the first full day of an Insight retreat focus on nothing more complicated than letting go of thoughts and summoning a simple mindfulness of breathing. Keeping the practice this simple can calm the mind and help with letting go of distracting thoughts. Trusting that this is all that is needed can help retreatants avoid succumbing to any sense of urgency or impatience.

By the second day, when meditators may be more settled, the instruction focuses on mindfulness of the body. Attention to the body can be difficult on the first day if there are many distracting thoughts or compelling emotions. Providing instructions on mindfulness of emotions or thinking on the second day can lead to more thinking. Because the body is not a thought, simple mindfulness of the body can help quiet our thinking.

On the third day, the instructions expand to include mindfulness of emotions. This follows the instruction on mindfulness of the body because it is much easier to be mindful of emotions if we know how to be aware of their present-moment physical sensations. Meditators may find it easier to avoid being pulled into any stories or commentary related to the emotions if they focus on the physical expression of an emotion. Mindfulness of emotions through mindfulness of the body is a way to be present with emotions in a radically simple way.

On the fourth day, the instruction focuses on mindfulness of thinking. If the thinking is less insistent at this point of the retreat, it can be easier to observe thoughts without being pulled into their content. We can metaphorically step back to watch thinking rather than getting involved in it. This then allows for a fuller understanding of different aspects of thinking—e.g., their emotional component, the energetic and compulsive forces that promote distraction, or fascination we may have with particular thoughts. By the fourth day, learning to be mindful of thinking may be possible, so the mind becomes quieter rather than "thought-full."

Through these first four days of instruction, breathing remains the default focus of attention if nothing else is more predominant. Mindfulness is only turned toward other physical sensations, emotions, or thinking when these become compelling. By otherwise returning over and over to breathing, breathing becomes a stabilizing influence in one's meditation practice, cultivating both concentration and mindfulness.

For seven-day retreats, the standard instruction may end on the fourth day after which teachers may provide varied guidance. Common is instruction in open awareness forms of mindfulness that may or may not include an intentional "anchor" for attention—i.e., a central focus such as breathing we return to when nothing else is calling attention. When awareness is stable enough in the present, mindfulness can remain receptive to whatever physical, emotional, or mental experiences arise in perception.

Another instruction on the last days of a retreat might be to notice the quality or attitude present in how one is aware, perhaps with an emphasis on keeping awareness relaxed, receptive, and free of attachments.

Buddhist meditation instructions aim to give meditators personal experience of Buddhist teachings, Insights, and liberations. Even though this is the case, when doing Insight practice, it is best to meditate without any active concern about attaining any goal. The focus of the basic instruction is to abide in a clear awareness of our present-moment, direct experience. Rather than trying to attain particular states of meditation, we first develop a clear, stable, equanimous, non-reactive awareness of our experience as it occurs. Equanimous awareness of our direct experience in the present opens the door to experiencing Buddhist teachings, Insights, and liberations.

4

The Buddha's Instruction

AN AUSPICIOUS DAY

Don't chase the past
Or long for the future.
The past is left behind;
The future, not yet reached.
Right here, where what is, have insight
Into phenomena that has arisen;
Knowing this unfalteringly and
Unshakeably, one develops the mind.
Ardently do what should be done today –
Who knows, death may come tomorrow.
There is no bargaining with death
And death's great army.
Whoever dwells thus ardent,
– active day and night –
Is, says the peaceful sage,
One who has an auspicious day.
                    —The Buddha

5

The Many Forms of Insight

The great variety of Vipassana meditation instruction is illustrated in Jack Kornfield's book *Living Dharma: Teachings and Meditation Instructions from Twelve Theravada Masters*, which describes the teachings of some of the great Thai and Burmese meditation masters of the twentieth century. Particularly important for the Western Insight Meditation teachers—which include the teachers of Insight Meditation Society, Spirit Rock, and the Insight Retreat Center—is the Vipassana practice taught by the Burmese meditation master Mahasi Sayadaw (1904-1982). To a great extent, the Mahasi-style meditation approach has been the basis for both Buddhist Insight and secular mindfulness movements. The Mahasi instruction lends itself to secular uses, partly because it is relatively easy to present without recourse to classic Buddhist teachings.

It was the Mahasi practice that Joseph Goldstein, Sharon Salzberg, and Jack Kornfield began teaching in the United States in the mid-1970s. Over time, these teachers, and the teachers they trained, adapted the basic Mahasi instruction. Some of these changes were made to better meet the needs of Western practitioners. Some were inspired by a variety of influences from inside and outside of Theravada Buddhism, such as Ajahn Chah, Krishnamurti, Gestalt therapy, Advaita Vedanta, the Tibetan Buddhist practice of Dzogchen, the concentration practices of the Theravada nun Ayya Khema and the Burmese monk Pa Auk Sayadaw, as well as the awareness practices of Zen and of the Burmese teacher U Tejaniya Sayadaw. Different Insight teachers vary in how these and other influences shape their instruction. Instructions also vary based on the teachings a teacher wants to emphasize and the purposes the instructions support at any given time.

6

Mindfulness of Breathing

"When mindfulness of breathing is developed and culti-vated, it is of great fruit and benefit. When mindfulness of breathing is developed and cultivated, it fulfills the four foundations of mindfulness. When the four foundations of mindfulness are developed and cultivated, they fulfill the seven factors of enlightenment. When the seven enlighten-ment factors are developed and cultivated, they fulfill true knowledge and liberation."

– The Buddha

After the Buddha returned from a three-month period of personal meditation, he explained that the practice he engaged in was mindfulness of breathing. From that time until today, mindfulness of breathing has been central for many Buddhist meditation practitioners. Not only has it been a vital thread passed down through the centuries, but it can also be a helpful "thread" running through a single meditation retreat. Having mindfulness of breathing as a constant through the days of a retreat can be the midline that keeps us from swinging too far from the balance and stability of present-moment attention.

Repeatedly returning the attention to breathing can decrease the mind's tendency to wander into the past or the future. It is a way to stay anchored in the present. On retreat, the instruction in mindfulness meditation usually begins by encouraging simple, easeful attention to breathing. Trying too hard to concentrate on the breath can often be counterproductive. Rather than straining to have 100% unwavering attention, it might be enough to pay attention to the breathing 60-70% of the time. This gives the mind ample opportunity to let go of distracting thoughts and begin again attending to the breath. Repeatedly letting go and starting again is a massage for the mind; slowly, the thinking mind relaxes and becomes less and less insistent. Thus, rather than forcing ourselves to concentrate, the art of mindfulness of breathing is repeatedly and pleasantly returning to it as soon as we see that the mind has wandered off. As the intensity of thinking decreases, the mind settles into a more focused, concentrated state without any strain.

The simplicity of retreat life, with its many hours of meditation, provides ample time for practicing mindfulness of breathing. If, throughout the day we can sustain attention on breathing for 60-70% of the time, this adds up to more concentration on breathing than we can usually sustain in daily life. If we also attend to our breathing outside the formal periods of meditation, it helps us settle more and more into the simplicity of being in the present. Standing in line waiting for a meal to start, eating the meal, sitting down to have a cup of tea, using the bathroom, and taking a stroll around the retreat property are all opportunities to check in with one's breathing. The idea is to steadily settle into attention that's unified on the experience of breathing.

On the way to developing a unification of mind, breathing can reveal a great deal about ourselves. Over the day, our breathing pattern may change depending on our state of mind, sometimes slower or faster, sometimes shallow or deep, sometimes coarse or subtle. Tension in the muscles used for breathing may vary in location and intensity depending on the thoughts and emotions present. It can be effective to gently continue breathing with whatever tension, emotions, or breathing pattern might be present. Maintaining continuity of attention on breathing with equanimity and non-reactivity is helpful because it loosens the mental link between our mind and muscles. Continuity of attention can give "breathing room" within which our tense muscles and emotions can come to relax. Giving attention to our breathing can protect us somewhat from our attention becoming preoccupied with interfering, judging, fixing, and reacting to what is happening.

Wandering off in thought is part of practicing mindfulness of breathing; there is no need to see it as a failure or a hindrance. Certainly, getting lost in thought for extended times is counterproductive in meditation. However, the rhythm of wandering off and returning gives us frequent opportunities to notice what prompts the mind to wander off. To notice this well, it's best to avoid jerking the attention back to the breath. Instead, we can let distraction serve as the occasion to understand what the mind is up to and the attitude behind our thinking. If the conditions of the mind that encourage wandering thoughts are not recognized, we are much more likely to wander off again. Taking a couple of moments to notice the nature of the wandering mind, we can try to relax any tension or pressure associated with thinking. Relaxing the "thinking muscle" tends to decrease the tendency to wander off into thought.

Furthermore, instead of hurrying to return our attention to breathing, we can take the time to let go back into the experience of breathing. Instead of pouncing back on the breathing or bearing down, relaxing into the felt sense of breathing might be more effective.

Once we are again attending to breathing, the practice skill is to sustain the attention. Here also, it's best to avoid trying too hard. Certainly, it's important to have the intention to maintain mindfulness on as many breaths in a row as we can. If we don't value the opportunity to do so, the mind is less likely to cooperate. One way to cultivate continuity is to focus the lens of attention so we have the clearest experience of breathing that's available. This asks us to do more than follow the rhythm of breathing in and out. It includes recognizing the sensations and physical movements in play as we breathe. It asks that we have a relaxed interest in discovering how each in-breath and out-breath is unique, with its texture and pattern of sensations. We can clearly feel the difference between the experiences of inhaling and exhaling. During part of the exhalation, there may be a natural letting go we can lightly emphasize. By allowing this letting go to continue for a nanosecond longer than it would on its own, concentration may begin to slowly strengthen.

As we take time to intimately experience breathing, we may begin to notice longer pauses at the end of an out-breath. If so, it can be helpful to let the pause linger gently and calmly, just long enough so the in-breath begins on its own. Perhaps we can surrender to the in-breath and receive it in awareness.

Tuning the lens of attention to inhaling can include noticing the growing pressure and expansion in the belly and chest as the lungs fill with air. Does this occur slowly or quickly? Does the expansion end suddenly, or does it slow down near the end? Can there be a surrender to the start of the exhalation?

As mindfulness of breathing grows, it can be helpful to notice at what points in the cycle of breathing the mind is most likely to wander off into thought. For some people, this is during the out-breath, often near the end. For some, it is in a gap at the end of the out-breath. And for others, it is during the in-breath. If we know there's a particular part of the cycle where we are likely to be pulled into thinking, we can then gently resolve to bring a heightened alertness at that point, vigilant not to wander away from breathing.

Retreats are a great time to become friends with your breathing. If you do, your breathing will befriend you. Over time, you will probably appreciate what a wonderful companion breathing can be, a companion to check in with throughout the day. Breathing can be a touchstone for a mindful life.

7

Doing One Thing at a Time

To develop meditation practice on retreat, we do just one thing at a time. Throughout the day, whatever you are doing, just do that one thing and nothing else. Give your attention wholly to the activity of the moment and see each activity through to its end. Avoid multitasking on retreat, as it fragments your attention. Instead, devote yourself to what you are doing; this will unify your attention.

If you are eating, focus on just eating. Eat without scanning the dining room to study how others are eating. Stay mindful of eating. Don't chew your food and think about issues in your life. Let chewing be the most valuable focus of the moment; think about your problems later. Instead of eating in a hurry, concerned with what is next, eat as if eating is your only concern. Wait to give your attention to what is next until it is time for what is next.

When walking somewhere, walk as if it is the only thing you need to do. Keep the focus on walking by not also looking around. If you want to scan the environment, stop walking, then look around. Similarly, refrain from staring at something while you are walking. This splitting of attention will weaken your mindfulness of walking. If you want to look, stop walking and allow looking to be the one thing you do. When finished looking, begin walking again. If you have decided to walk from point A to point B, don't veer off to point C. Follow through on what you started. After getting to B, you can go to C. While this way of walking isn't always necessary for daily life, it builds the continuity of mindfulness on retreat.

Doing one thing at a time during ordinary activities on retreat strengthens your ability to do the same in meditation—that is, to simply meditate when meditating. Training attention in any activity increases your capacity for attention in meditation.

A valuable way to do one thing at a time is to practice embodied attention with what you are doing. Engage with a posture that allows your whole body to feel involved in the activity. When washing your dishes, be grounded in your body and have both hands equally dedicated to the washing. When mindfulness is rooted in somatic awareness, it tends to be more stable and supported.

Avoid doing things halfheartedly or non-committedly. Your life is too important to do anything distractedly or partially. Any activity you do provides an opportunity, right then and there, to wake up. Nearly any retreat activity can be an occasion to let go of any resistance or reluctance you might have in doing the activity. You can discover peace and liberation in whatever you are doing.

By regularly practicing one thing at a time, you will gradually become familiar with the benefits of this simplicity. You may feel what it is like for the body and mind to work together in harmony. You may appreciate being more settled, and less entangled with your thoughts. This familiarity is helpful for meditation. Recognizing the first hints of calm and harmonious feelings can serve as biofeedback, guiding you to stay focused on your meditation.

As we practice doing one thing at a time, we begin to understand the disadvantages of being preoccupied with thinking. More and more, we can become less interested in distracting thoughts. Being aware becomes more enjoyable than being distracted.

When doing one thing at a time is challenging, it is beneficial to discover what emotions, impulses, desires, and thoughts fuel the challenge. Learning this outside of meditation will prepare you to apply this learning to your meditation. Train yourself to identify which distractions, preoccupations, or reactivities are useless to pursue and which can be important subjects for mindful attention.

One of the fruits of mature meditation practice is enjoying the attention to doing one thing at a time.

Before this fruit ripens, practicing one thing at a time is the seed that, if watered, develops into this deep satisfaction with being present for everything we do, including meditation.

8

The Dharma of Hand Washing

The ordinary activities of daily life provide easy opportunities for practicing mindfulness and compassion. Hand washing is one of these, as it is an opportunity to be mindful through our whole being while also caring for others. When we're dedicated and intent on practicing while standing at the sink, our body, hands, and the flowing water then become our "meditation hall," "retreat center," or even "temple."

Taking time to wash our hands mindfully can be an occasion to notice if we are in a hurry, distracted, or dismissive of the value of being present for a mundane activity. It is an opportunity to experience the satisfaction of simply doing one activity. Surely, during the twenty seconds washing, it is okay to let go of other concerns. These few seconds are enough time to become grounded, centered, and calm in our daily life.

Just as mindfulness of breathing doesn't end after a single session of meditation, the simple practice of mindful hand washing is not something we ever finish. It's endlessly enriching each time we practice it.

Hand washing is a way to care for others. Colds and flu spread through our hands. Even if you aren't sick, your hands can easily pick up germs you then pass on. Avoiding passing on illness is a simple way to support our communities; it is a crucial protection for people with compromised immune systems.

Repeated and thorough hand washing can be a vehicle for developing our mindfulness and compassion. The following Buddhist verse expresses this dual role; reciting it three times takes about 20 seconds!

> *Cleaning my hands,*
> *I clean my heart and mind.*
> *Cleaning my heart and mind,*
> *I clean the world for others.*

9

Instructions for Walking Meditation

Most people in the West associate meditation with sitting quietly. But traditional Buddhist teachings identify four meditation postures: sitting, walking, standing, and lying down. All four are suitable means of cultivating a calm and clear mindfulness of the present moment. The most common meditation posture after sitting is walking. Meditation centers and monasteries have indoor halls and outdoor paths designated for walking meditation. Regular walking meditation is an integral part of the schedule on meditation retreats. In practice outside of retreats, some people will include walking as part of their daily meditation practice, for example, ten or twenty minutes before sitting meditation, or doing walking meditation instead of sitting.

Walking meditation brings many benefits in addition to the cultivation of mindfulness. It can be a helpful way of building concentration in support of sitting practice. When we are tired or sluggish, walking can be invigorating. The sensations of walking can be more compelling than the more subtle sensations of breathing while sitting. Walking can be helpful after a meal, waking from sleep, or after a long period of sitting meditation. Walking meditation may be more relaxing than sitting during times of strong emotions or stress. An added benefit is that walking meditation can build strength and stamina when done for extended periods.

People have a variety of attitudes toward walking meditation. Some take to it quickly and find it a delight. For many others, an appreciation of this form of meditation takes some time; it's an "acquired taste." Yet others see its benefits and do walking meditation even though they don't have much taste for it.

To do formal walking meditation, we find a pathway about 20 to 40 paces long and walk back and forth. If we're walking slowly, when we reach the end of our path, we come to a complete stop, turn around, stop again, and then start walking again. For the most part, we keep our eyes cast down without looking at anything. Some people find it helpful to keep the eyelids half closed. If we're walking at a faster pace, instead of stopping when we reach the end of our path, we can gracefully spin around as a continuity of the movement of walking. When walking fast, it might be better to have the eyes more open with a loose focus in front of you.

Walking back and forth on a single path is more helpful than wandering about because when we're wandering, part of the mind is busy negotiating the route. Some amount of mental effort is required to avoid a chair or step over a rock. When you walk back and forth, you quickly know the route, and the problem-solving part of the mind can rest.

Walking in a circle is a technique for walking meditation, but the disadvantage is that the continuity of a circle can conceal a wandering mind. Walking back and forth—and the interruption that occurs when we stop at the end of our path—can help to catch our attention if it has wandered.

As you walk back and forth, find a pace that gives you a sense of ease. I recommend walking more slowly than normal, but the speed can vary. Fast walking may bring greater ease when you are agitated. Fast walking is also appropriate when you are sleepy. Slow walking may feel more natural when the mind is calm and alert. Your speed might change during a period of walking meditation. See if you can sense the pace that keeps you most intimate with and attentive to the physical experience of walking. After you've found a pace of ease, let your attention settle into the body. I sometimes find it restful to think of letting my body take me for a walk.

Once you feel connected to the body, let your attention settle into your feet and lower legs. Sitting meditation commonly uses the alternating sensations of breathing in and out as an "anchor" keeping us in the present. In walking meditation, the focus is on the alternating steps of the feet.

With your attention on the legs and feet, feel the sensations of each step. Notice how the legs and feet tense as you lift the leg. Feel the movement of the leg swinging through the air. Feel the contact of the foot with the ground. There is no "right" experience to have. Just see how the experience feels to you. Whenever you notice that the mind has wandered, bring it back to the sensations of the feet walking. Getting a sense of the rhythm of the steps may help maintain a continuity of awareness.

As an aid to staying present, you can use a quiet mental label for your steps as you walk. The label might be "stepping, stepping" or "left, right." Labeling occupies the thinking mind with a rudimentary form of thought, so the mind is less likely to wander off. The labeling also points the awareness toward what you want to observe. Noting "stepping" helps you to notice the feet. If, after a while, you notice that you are saying "right" for the left foot and "left" for the right foot, you know that your attention has wandered.

When walking more slowly, you might try breaking each step into phases and using the traditional labels "lifting, placing." For very slow walking, you can use the labels "lifting, moving, placing" to divide each step into three phases.

Try to dedicate your attention to the sensations of walking and let go of everything else. If powerful emotions or thoughts arise and call your attention away from the sensations of walking, it's often helpful to stop walking and attend to them. You can return to walking meditation when they are no longer compelling. If something beautiful or interesting catches your eye while walking, stop walking and do "looking" meditation. Continue walking when you have finished looking.

Some people find their minds more active or distractible during walking than sitting meditation. This may be because walking is more active, and the eyes are open. If so, don't be discouraged and think walking meditation is useless. It's often more beneficial than we realize at the moment.

We spend more time walking in our daily lives than sitting quietly with closed eyes. Walking meditation can be a powerful bridge between meditation practice and everyday life, helping us be more present, mindful, and concentrated in ordinary activities. It can reconnect us to a simplicity of being and the wakefulness that comes from it.

10

Mindful Postures

When walking, one knows one is walking;
When standing, one knows one is standing;
When sitting, one knows one is sitting;
When lying down, one knows one is lying down.
— *the Buddha*

Mindfulness of posture is a beneficial part of the Buddhist path to liberation. We can learn to avoid postures that undermine us and move into postures that help us feel empowered and free. At first, we can do this intentionally. As awareness and inner freedom become stronger, skillful postures become less something we assume and more something that arises naturally from our practice.

"Mindfulness of postures" is an essential foundation for meditation. Our capacities for stability, confidence, and resiliency can be more readily available when we assume postures that give these qualities a chance to appear. Mindful postures enhance awareness of our body by bringing a greater sense of embodiment or "body-fulness" to our mindfulness. In addition, they help prevent unnecessary discomfort in meditation.

Attention to posture is beneficial during meditation retreats, where we may stay with a particular posture continuously for longer than we usually do in daily life.

When meditating, we can bring attention to our posture in three general ways. First, we can use attention to posture as a window to our inner life — to our emotions, attitudes, and intentions. Second, we can assume postures that bring physical and psychological benefits that support meditation practice. And third, we can find postures that avoid unnecessary physical discomfort. This can allow us to meditate for longer periods without having to work with pain.

Self-understanding Through Posture

Twenty-four hours a day, we assume a wide array of postures, sometimes consciously, most often unconsciously. Because posture often expresses attitudes and emotions we are experiencing, attention to it can bring a greater awareness of our underlying mindsets, moods, and feelings. For example, emotions like fear, anger, and resistance are expressed in our posture quite differently than happiness, confidence, and determination. With some attitudes, the body pulls in, collapses, or tightens up. With others, it opens, expands, and relaxes.

During meditation, subtle shifts in posture can arise out of aspects of our psychological state. Straining in meditation can result in a tightening of the body. Resistance may be felt as a pulling back. Expectation and anticipation may come with a slight leaning forward. Complacency

with meditation can manifest in a sinking posture. Calm
enthusiasm for practice can show itself in a relaxed, alert
posture. Contentment and happiness may come with a
sense of lightening and uplift.

With regular meditation practice, we can become
increasingly familiar with the subtle variations in our meditation posture and the way these variations express how
we feel. This is particularly so when we first sit down to
meditate. We may be leaning, twisting, or slouching more
than usual. Our moods, attitudes, and sense of vitality may
be reflected in how upright we sit, how open the chest is,
how and where the body is tense, which muscles don't
relax, and what parts of the body feel energized.

Posture as a Support for Practice

A mindful meditation posture can provide many more
benefits than simply allowing us to be physically comfortable during a meditation session. It is possible to assume
postures that support mindfulness, concentration, and
other useful psychological states. Through attention to
posture, our bodies can participate in the practice of meditation, making meditation much more than a mental
activity.

The attention required to take an intentional posture—i.e., an upright posture that takes some ongoing

attention to maintain— is a support for both mindfulness and concentration. Ideally, such a posture would also provide a strong, stable base against the floor, cushion, or chair. Over time, the intention to assume this posture becomes second nature and seemingly effortless.

A reciprocal relationship exists between our bodies and our mental states. Whatever mood our posture expresses is reinforced by the posture itself. If we slump when sad, the slumping can strengthen the sadness. If we assume an upright, strong, stable posture, we are less likely to increase the sorrow; instead, we may be able to attend to it with stable, respectful awareness. When anxiety manifests in a tight chest, we're less likely to be under its influence if we sit up straight with the chest broad and the shoulders rolled back. We may be able to call forth the courage to face it directly.

The traditional instruction is to meditate with a posture that expresses dignity. Even if we don't feel it, we may benefit from sitting in a dignified posture, with an upright, balanced torso and a relaxed face, belly, and hands. When we do this, a forgotten or buried sense of dignity may have a chance to surface. The many statues of the Buddha meditating provide an example of a posture that expresses a quiet dignity, perhaps even a soft regality. It can serve as a model for a posture of relaxed confidence, gentle strength, and non-entangled awareness.

It can be very supportive on meditation retreats to assume an easy upright posture throughout the day. By doing this while sitting, standing, walking, and lying down, we counter the influence of debilitating attitudes. We are more likely to call on our reservoirs of confidence.

Mitigating Discomfort

Finding a personally appropriate posture to avoid unnecessary discomfort when meditating is important. No posture will be suitable for everyone. And no posture will always remain the proper posture for any one person over time. For this reason, it's helpful to know a range of postural options and learn to adjust as needed. Becoming skilled in meditating in various postures gives us greater flexibility and adaptability with our meditation. It facilitates alternating between postures during meditation retreats.

It is beneficial to receive instruction in meditation posture from various teachers, each of whom may know different aspects of suitable postures for meditation. Because so many physical details go into meditation posture, even longtime meditators with a comfortable posture can often benefit from hearing posture instruction.

Sometimes it's helpful to have another person look at your meditation posture. Someone else may see aspects of your posture you can't see or feel yourself. They may be able to point out where your posture is out of balance. Some people will feel themselves sitting completely straight while meditating even though their torso is leaning, or their head is tilted. Any lean or tilt will build a strain over time.

While being comfortable in meditation is helpful, it's important not to use physical comfort as the only criterion for our meditation posture. This is most relevant when what may be comfortable in the short term perpetuates unhelpful postural habits in the long term. It may also prevent the strengthening of muscles that support good posture. Also, at times, discomfort may signal the release of muscular tension, so avoiding such pain can interfere with further release and relaxation. In such circumstances, it's helpful to continue to sit and practice with discomfort rather than avoiding it. Other times it's appropriate to shift the posture only enough that the discomfort becomes manageable as a good subject for mindfulness.

Careful mindfulness of physical discomfort can sometimes provide us with important information. It can also help us understand whether the discomfort might cause an injury. While it's rare to get injured from meditation, it can happen, especially when meditators force themselves to endure pain without careful attention. In general, a potentially injurious pain will feel different from pain that is non-injurious. There will be a "danger" signal connected with detrimental pain. If the pain arouses any suspicion of possible injury, it's important to move. And if it's unclear whether continuing with physical pain may cause harm, it's best to change your posture to alleviate the discomfort. One clear sign that a meditation posture is injurious is if physical pain connected to meditation continues for more than five minutes after getting up from a meditation session.

Regular meditation practice is a way to develop a meditation posture that brings ongoing benefits. Slowly, the body will settle in, build strength, and release tension that establishes a supportive meditation posture. Equally slowly, we can develop a greater body awareness that supports a good posture. Sometimes a body that has settled into an upright, dignified meditation posture is called a "yogic body," a form of posture that can bring a level of integration such that the entire body feels harmonized into a peaceful, energized whole.

11

Retreat Practice Wisdom

A meditator's toolbox can hold a variety of "wisdom perspectives" that we can bring out whenever useful. These function as antidotes to unwise perspectives. What follows are some points of view I have found helpful for retreat practice.

"Every Moment of Mindfulness Is Beneficial"

While, at times, mindfulness practice may not appear to provide any benefits, Insights, or positive feedback, each moment of mindfulness is beneficial. In the same way that many continuous drops of water can slowly fill a bathtub, our individual moments of mindfulness add up and build and strengthen our capacities over time.

Sometimes it's obvious that being mindful is better than anything else the mind might be doing. Each moment of mindfulness counteracts forces of preoccupation in the mind and may be keeping it out of trouble. Each moment of mindfulness weakens the negative mental habits reinforced over many moments—if not hours or years—of distraction. Each moment of mindfulness also strengthens the mental "muscle" of mindfulness so that our ability to be mindful is ready for more challenging times.

There's a saying that it's too late to dig a well when the house is on fire. Similarly, it may be too late to start meditating when we are in a crisis. A well-developed meditation practice prepares us for times of challenge. To develop our mindfulness, it's helpful to remember that "every moment of mindfulness is beneficial; no act of mindfulness is ever wasted."

"Right on Time"

Any difficulty can be used to develop mindfulness, wisdom, and Insight. To get the most out of mindfulness, view every difficulty as arising "right on time" for your practice. Rather than protesting or despairing, approach everything that happens on retreat as presenting you with the right practice opportunity for the current moment.

You might imagine looking at a wristwatch while thinking, "right on time!" This perspective is a reminder that nothing is a distraction; there is only the next thing we include as part of the practice. To view each arising experience as simply the next thing to meet with mindfulness can lead to great equanimity. It is a view that provides a kind of infinite forgiveness for any personal challenges we may find ourselves having in the retreat; instead of lingering with self-recrimination, we dedicate ourselves to remaining in the flow of present-moment awareness.

"I Am Responsible for Myself; Others Are Responsible for Themselves"

This saying encourages us to avoid preoccupation with what other retreatants are doing or not doing. Taking responsibility for other people's retreat practice interferes with our practice. It may even interfere with theirs. It is wiser to remember that each retreatant's task is to practice as wisely as possible with whatever arises on the retreat. Whether or how others do this does not need to be our responsibility.

In leaving each person answerable to themselves for their choices in how to practice, we allow them to learn the lessons they may need. At the same time, we strengthen our ability to be undistracted.

Not taking responsibility for others is not the same as being aloof or indifferent. It is giving people freedom from our over-involvement and over-judgmentalism. It also allows people to do the inner work that only they can do. Every person matures on the path of liberation by attending to their inner life; on retreat, it is best to focus on your own.

If you're on retreat with a relative or friend, please discuss together before the start of the retreat how to leave each other alone, so each is responsible for themselves.

"Whether We Know It or Not, We Practice for the Benefit of All"

Not taking responsibility for how others practice doesn't mean we need to be unconcerned with their welfare. Buddhist practice reveals we are all profoundly and mutually interconnected; we are all kin to each other. We can learn from one another, inspire one another, and realize how much the path of liberation is interpersonal as much as personal.

When we engage in our practice, even if we believe we are doing it to heal and resolve our suffering, our practice benefits others. On retreat, each person's dedicated practice supports the practice of the group. Each person's growth and transformation through the practice can inspire others to practice. Furthermore, each person's resolution of their inner demons makes them a better member of our human family. People maturing on the Buddhist path evolve ethically; they become refuges of safety for others. Knowing our practice benefits others even when we do not actively intend this can give added motivation to practice.

"The Dharma Knows Better Than We Do What We Need to Practice"

Sometimes retreatants come to retreat with expectations about how they will practice, what issues they will be working on, and what will happen. Most commonly, the retreat unfolds differently from these expectations. Unanticipated physical experiences appear; surprising emotions emerge; unforeseen concerns and memories loom large. Some are underlying thought patterns and emotional attitudes, invisible in daily life, that are important to see. In general, the more challenged we feel by something that has arisen, the more likely it is that something deep in us has been aroused and needs our attention. If these are attachments, sooner or later, they need to be included as part of the practice.

The perspective that "the Dharma knows better than you what you need to practice" is a view that encourages us to practice with everything that occurs as if there are lessons to learn, attachments to shed, or wholesome mind states to bring forth. We don't need to know why something is happening; we only need to accept it as a worthy focus of practice.

As the practice allows us to experience our potential for ease, peace, and kindness, we become increasingly sensitive to how our views affect our well-being. While some views may distance us from this potential, others may be in harmony with it, perhaps even arising from the vision this ease, peace, and kindness provide. It is helpful to remember the understandings that come from this inner vision. Some of the aphorisms offered in this essay may be useful. And sometimes, when the vision of freedom and kindness is clear enough, we won't need positive views; we only need to see clearly.

12

Community as Part of Retreat Practice

An essential aspect of residential retreats is practicing in a community of other practitioners. Meditation, listening to dharma talks, eating meals, and engaging in some work assignments all occur with others. In monasteries without single rooms, even sleeping is done in close proximity to others.

Practicing in community, we benefit from the inspiration others can provide. Experienced practitioners can provide newer practitioners with examples of how to engage wholeheartedly in retreat life. Seeing the steadiness, kindness, calmness, and mindfulness of others can inspire us to call on these qualities in ourselves.

Meditating with others can be deeply encouraging. On their own, many people would not have the personal discipline or inspiration to maintain a meditation schedule throughout the day; meditating with others can make it much easier to keep going. This is especially true when doubt, inertia, and other meditation challenges occur. The silent support of fellow meditators can encourage us, providing the needed boost to work through challenges.

Practicing with others makes it clear that we are not alone in practice. Because meditation—and retreat practice especially—is an unusual activity in our culture, knowing that others are doing it can counter any concerns we might have that we're doing something odd or abnormal. Whether our meditation is going well or we're experiencing difficulties, practicing with others can protect us from thinking we are special or unique: we're surrounded by others who may be experiencing the same things. Knowing this helps us understand that our experiences are a normal part of the spiritual journey, to be met with mindfulness, wise humility, and compassion.

To practice as a community is to practice with the attitude that we are all in the retreat together. We participate in the retreat both for our own benefit and for the benefit of others. We care for ourselves when we care for others, and we can care for others to care for ourselves. How much we emphasize one side of this dynamic process varies from retreat to retreat. Sometimes the focus of practice is more personal; other times, it is actively serving the other retreatants. For example, one may want to participate as a retreat manager or retreat cook, both significant ways of practicing on retreat where the focus is on serving others.

Practicing in a community provides direct lessons in how we live in mutual support with others. When everyone helps with the chores of the retreat, we both support others and are supported by them. Experiencing these areas of mutual support can help us relax as we learn we are not alone as we walk a path to freedom amid our social relationships. It points to our profound interconnectedness within which we find freedom from emotional interdependency.

Living and practicing in silence with others during a retreat allows for unique and wonderful connections between us. Because we don't engage in social conversation, people on retreat tend to become aware of each other in new ways. During the many circumstances when we are with others in silence, closeness, familiarity, and appreciation grow without speaking. Small interactions like opening the door for each other, sharing a meal, washing dishes together, and spending hours meditating near each other in the meditation hall give birth to mutual appreciation.

People accustomed to being alone or acculturated to individualism may not appreciate how important community life is to retreat practice. For some phases of Buddhist practice, the community aspects of practice can even become the most important. Practicing in community is an antidote to the hyper-individualism that is all too common in our culture. To be too focused on one's own practice and happiness paradoxically limits the growth of that practice and happiness. Being mindful of and caring for others softens hard boundaries between self and other people. Finding harmony in living with others teaches valuable lessons in non-clinging.

Of course, living in proximity to others can have challenges. Fellow retreatants can be distracting. They can be noisy or inconsiderate. Romantic attractions and hostile aversions may occur. Concerns about what others think about us may be preoccupying. But rather than taking these challenges as unwanted, they are best seen as material to practice with, as opportunities to find inner peace independent of what is happening around us. The simplicity, calm, and heightened mindfulness of retreat life facilitate working through some of the common interpersonal issues that are so common in daily life. It can lead to a freedom where our well-being is not dependent on how others behave.

Appreciating the role of community expands the value of meditation retreats. Practicing in community supports a growth of inner freedom that goes together with an increase in interpersonal warmth and compassion.

13

The Silence of Silent Retreats

Silence is a prominent feature of most Insight meditation retreats. While on retreat, participants are silent for extended periods, often far longer than in any other situation they've been in. Once the retreat begins, retreatants agree to limit their talking solely to necessary speech, such as speaking to a teacher during practice discussion or asking a question during work meditation. In addition, they have only a few occasions to hear anyone else talk. The result is a pervasive silence that serves as a foundation for the meditation practice and can hopefully create a palpable and nourishing atmosphere of stillness.

Silence can be challenging for some people at the beginning of their first retreat. Because it is a new and unfamiliar experience, retreat silence can be confusing. This is especially true when a person's primary associations with silence are uncomfortable—for example, when their only experience of social silence is loneliness or exclusion.

Most people, however, come to cherish the silence of retreat. Even those intimidated by it in the beginning often find enough peace in the silence they are reluctant to give it up at the end. As people become aware of its richness, they look forward to silence rather than fear it.

Retreat silence has many benefits. Because social conversation keeps the mind active, periods of not talking can help the mind to quiet. Silence settles the many emotions activated by talking, anticipating conversations, or even listening. As our mental and emotional lives calm down, our bodies relax.

Silence allows for a heightened sense of intimacy with the world. In sustained silence, our senses become more acute, and the inner and outer worlds can appear to us with greater clarity. For example, we may notice the birdsong we previously failed to hear or tune in to our quieter thoughts, which generally get drowned out.

The primary reason for silence on meditation retreats is to support our meditation practice. Silence helps keep our focus on cultivating mindfulness and concentration. Continuity of mindfulness is much easier when we don't talk. The complex interplay of emotions and attitudes involved in most social interactions tends to keep the mind too active and scattered to allow for deep concentration. And this internal activity often lingers. The mental momentum from a conversation can continue after we stop talking. It can take a while for the thinking mind to quiet down after a conversation ends.

For most people, the silence of a retreat creates a space in which they can see themselves more clearly. Rather than being actively distracted by work, relationships, the internet, music, or various external events, they have an opportunity to notice overlooked feelings and concerns. The sustained periods of silence allow people to observe the subtle, important motivations and values behind how they live.

Retreats are also a great place to discover what Buddhism calls "noble silence." This beautiful state of mind comes when discursive thinking has stopped. Discursive thinking is thinking that proceeds like an inner discourse in our minds. It may be imagining conversations with others, remembering past conversations, or talking to ourselves. It may involve abstract, analytical thinking about what is happening in the present moment. As discursive thinking quiets down, the mind becomes more peaceful. As agitation decreases, desire and aversion lessen. When this inner stilling is accompanied by confidence, purity, and equanimity, the mind is said to experience the fullness of "noble silence."

Because Insight meditation retreats are group retreats, practitioners spend a lot of time in silence alongside others. As they relax into the collective stillness, participants often discover that being together with others in silence allows for a rich sense of connection that is more satisfying than if they had spent the same time engaged in conversation. Rather than knowing others through the stories of who they are and what they have done, the silence highlights our shared humanity and a natural feeling of empathy and rapport. A wonderful lesson from a retreat is how the quiet ways of being with others can allow for a deep sense of connection.

As people discover the great value of retreat silence, they can explore the uses of silence in daily life. Learning to be comfortable with silence expands what is possible in our relationships—both with others and ourselves. Spending time in silence can enrich both. It can be a great support in helping us discover greater spiritual freedom wherever we are. And with freedom, we can experience stillness and peace even in speech.

14

Renunciation

The Buddhist path is often considered one of renunciation. Retreats are a form of temporary renunciation. The purpose is not to deprive retreatants of anything, it is to create the best conditions to walk the Buddhist path. In the same way that a path cleared in a jungle allows ease of movement through the thick vegetation, putting aside everyday concerns and activities clears the way through the thick overgrowth of life's complications.

That renunciation is part of Buddhism is easy to see in the lifestyle of simplicity and restraint followed by Buddhist monastics. The role of renunciation in the lives of lay practitioners is more challenging to understand. Lay practitioners are usually not asked to renounce money, sex, intoxicants, and entertainment. So, it can be a surprise to learn this is expected on Insight meditation retreats. The lifestyle on these retreats is more monastic than what is typically associated with lay life.

Because so many people have serious reservations about the idea of doing without, Buddhist teachers in America are sometimes reluctant to teach about renunciation. Indeed, there are good reasons to be suspicious of appeals to let go. For example, renunciation may be confused with aversion or repression instead of an impulse of freedom. When it's overdone, renunciation may blind us to our real needs and healthy motivations. Or renunciation may be burdened with puritanical notions of good and bad, purity and impurity. Most importantly, we may confuse the renouncing of things and experiences (like money, sex, and possessions) with the essential work of renouncing our clinging to them.

The Latin root of the word sacrifice means "to make sacred." The Buddha did not teach renunciation as a form of denial or asceticism. Instead, he taught letting go as a way to achieve a greater good, greater happiness, and ultimately to attain what might be called the "sacred" dimension of liberation. The Buddha once said, "If one sees that a greater happiness is found by letting go of a lesser one, the wise person will let go of the lesser happiness."

Even though it doesn't take much mindfulness to recognize that suffering comes with clinging, we often find it hard to let go of clinging or to see letting go as possible or worthwhile. Strong feelings of desire often come with a compulsion that makes the desire seem necessary. Or we may approach clinging like a lottery—we are willing to bear the risk of suffering in exchange for the chance that the clinging will bring us well-being. Furthermore, letting go can be frightening. Clinging may give us a sense of taking care of ourselves; holding tight to security, judgments, people, self-identity, or possessions are all ways of protecting ourselves. People may only know how to function in the world with the motivation and self-identity that come from clinging.

Renunciation is often difficult. Grappling with the power of desire, attachments, and fear may require great personal struggle. But that struggle yields many benefits. We develop the inner strength to overcome temptation and compulsion. We don't have to live with the suffering and contraction that come with clinging. Clinging can be exhausting; letting go is restful. We may taste the luminous mind of freedom hidden when clinging is present. And, finally, we are more available to work for the welfare of others.

Renunciation should bring joy or at least a lightness of being. If it's done with resentment or resistance, then the renunciation is not thorough—some clinging remains. We may need time on retreat to understand what we still have to let go of. If the heart is still pining, if the mind is still tight or hot, then the renunciation is incomplete.

Suzuki Roshi once defined renunciation as accepting that things change and pass away. This definition points to two things. First, sometimes renunciation takes the form of wise surrender to the unavoidable. Second, at its heart, the practice of renunciation requires an inner release that may or may not require letting go of anything external. External renunciation without a corresponding inner release may strengthen clinging. Relinquishing something without releasing the desire is a condition for suffering.

One of the primary functions of a retreat's renunciation of so many aspects of ordinary life is facilitating inner transformation. Realizing that what we assumed was necessary for happiness is, in fact, not required (and may not even be a cause of happiness after all) can bring a marvelous sense of ease. On retreat, we give up speech, entertainment, reading, writing, sexual activity, and much of our control over what we eat. In surrendering to the retreat schedule, we give up our preferences for what we do and when. If these limitations are difficult, the difficulties become an opportunity for spiritual practice. When we see renunciation not as a limitation but as unburdening, we can take great delight in feeling free from desire and compulsion.

Renunciation on retreat is a practice worth practicing. You can learn a lot about what would be good to renounce in daily life. Maybe your opinions? Maybe self-preoccupation? Or a strong desire? In what areas of your life would letting go bring greater benefits than continuing to hold on tightly? When letting go is difficult, what does your clinging indicate about your beliefs about what will make you happy?

Are there things or activities in your life that would be good to do without or to limit? For example, watching television, shopping, complaining, gossiping, constantly checking electronic devices, surfing the web? For some, being overly busy is an important area for letting go. There are many worthwhile pursuits; trying to do too many is harmful. Sometimes it is necessary to choose which is most important to us and then let the rest go.

To sacrifice is to make sacred. To release is to find freedom. And to find freedom is to know a happiness that is not dependent on anything—especially not on having our wishes fulfilled.

15

Practicing with the Retreat Schedule

Most meditation retreats have a schedule that includes the primary activities of each day. Posted in prominent places around the retreat center, the schedule indicates times for meditation throughout the day as well as the wake-up bell, meals, and teachings offered. Listing activities that occur regularly throughout the day, the schedule is a companion to everyone on the retreat. It provides a supportive scaffolding for retreat life.

Every retreatant has a relationship with the schedule. People new to retreats are often surprised it fills so much of the day. Those with retreat experience often arrive with attitudes and intentions regarding the schedule based on previous retreats. Throughout a retreat most people's relationship with the schedule shifts. This can include a wide assortment of emotional reactions: from feeling content and supported to being intimidated and resistant. Our attitude can influence how much or how little we participate in the scheduled activities.

Our relationship to the schedule is an important part of retreat practice and can be a valuable topic of discussion with a teacher. Rather than seeing it as an arbitrary or neutral backdrop for our meditation, the schedule is integral to the practice of the retreat. As such, it can teach us about ourselves, help us develop inner strengths, and support the discovery of greater freedom.

The Schedule as a Mirror

An important foundation for Buddhist practice is understanding the underlying beliefs, desires, and reactions that motivate our mental, physical, and verbal behavior. When unseen, these can operate in the background, subconsciously affecting all areas of our lives. When they're recognized and known, however, we can investigate and address them with wisdom. Most importantly, we can discover inner freedom in relating to them.

The retreat schedule can be a mirror for understanding ourselves better. Observing how we participate with the schedule can provide Insight into attitudes, beliefs, motivations, and feelings that can go unseen if we are free of any timetable. If we are chronically late for scheduled events, we can ask, "why?" If we regularly wait until the last moment to show up for a scheduled event, why? If we always arrive early, why? If we resist schedules, why? The following questions can support self-discovery:

- What is your general attitude about the schedule?
- Do you consider the schedule helpful?

- Do you have any enthusiasm or anxiety about participating in the schedule?
- Do you approach the schedule as a rigid requirement or as an optional suggestion?
- What emotions and motivations influence how you follow the schedule? Are these emotions and motivations characterized more by ease or by tension?
- What role do expectations and imagined consequences have in how you follow a schedule?
- When the schedule challenges you, how can this challenge become a subject for greater mindfulness or self-awareness?
- When following the schedule feels effortless, what does it teach you about freedom?

Developing Strengths

An important aspect of retreat practice is developing our inner strengths and character, so they support us along the path of mindfulness. How we participate in the schedule can influence this inner growth. Sometimes adhering to the schedule can develop discipline, patience, and equanimity. Other times, deviating from the schedule can cultivate discernment, self-reliance, and autonomy. Sometimes, following the schedule can free us from needing to decide what to do. This, in turn, can facilitate calm, steadiness, and letting go. Other times, it is choosing not to follow the full schedule that provides calm, steadiness, and letting go.

A Vehicle for Freedom

Buddhist practice reveals the freedom of an unfettered heart––a freedom that manifests in our relationship to everything we encounter inside and outside of ourselves. With freedom we discover an abiding ease, free of greed, hate, anxiety, or delusion. The schedule of a retreat facilitates this freedom by supporting an ongoing continuity of practice and by being something with which we learn to be free.

Buddhist liberation is primarily freedom from attachment rather than freedom to do what we want. Doing what we want may be motivated by attachments and aversions. One way to use a retreat schedule is to avoid acting on preferences and compulsions.

For this reason, following the retreat schedule as posted is useful. The schedule has been designed based on many years of experience as to what works well for both individuals and for groups practicing together. Persisting with the schedule can ensure a continuity of practice through all the ups and downs we might go through while on retreat. It also provides an opportunity to learn how to be free amid all the ups and downs. Skipping parts of the schedule too readily can lead us to miss this opportunity.

However, sometimes it can be helpful to diverge from the posted schedule. For example, sometimes taking a break from the schedule is the best support for the continuity of the practice when it allows us to return to the practice refreshed.

Sometimes, extending sitting or walking meditation beyond the scheduled time allows for a deeper settling. By adjusting the schedule for themselves, some people free themselves from a tendency to obedience, always trying to do the "right" thing, or fearing judgment from others when not following the norm.

The retreat schedule has a vital role in the community life of everyone on a retreat. Everyone is connected to the schedule. By participating in the schedule, we support others to do the same. Because of this, when we diverge from the schedule, we can consider how to do this, so it doesn't undermine this support. True freedom is not found in ignoring the well-being of others, but rather in developing a heart where care for others is an integral part of freedom. The retreat schedule is in service of the greatest good for all who participate in a retreat.

16

IRC Weeklong Retreat Schedule

OPENING DAY

- 1:00 to 3:00 pm Check-in
- 4:30 pm Orientation in Community Room
- 5:30 pm Supper
- 7:30 pm Opening Session in Meditation Hall
- 9:00 pm Sleep or further practice

BASIC DAILY SCHEDULE

- 5:30 am Wake-up
- 6:00 am Sit
- 6:40 am Sangha Service
- 7:00 am Breakfast
- 7:30 am Work meditation for some
- 8:30 am Sit with Instructions followed by Walking Instructions
- 9:30 am Walk
- 10:15 am Sit
- 11:00 am Walk or Posture Instructions
- 11:45 am Sit
- 12:15 pm Lunch
- 12:45 pm Work meditation for some
- 1:45 pm Sit
- 2:30 pm Walk
- 3:15 pm Sit

- 3:50 pm Walk or Stretch
- 4:00 pm Dharma Talk
- 5:00 pm Walk
- 5:30 pm Supper
- 6:00 pm Work meditation for some
- 6:45 pm Sit
- 7:15 pm Walk
- 7:45 pm Sit
- 8:30 pm Walk
- 9:00 pm Sit
- 9:30 pm Sleep or further practice

CLOSING DAY SCHEDULE

- 5:30 am Wake-up
- 6:00 am Sit
- 6:40 am Sangha Service
- 7:00 am Breakfast
- 7:30 am Work meditation for some, room cleaning & packing for others
- 8:30 am Sit, announcements
- 9:00 am Walk or Personal room cleaning and packing
- 9:45 am Final Sit
- 10:15 am Cleaning of Center
- 11:15 am Closing Meeting in Community Room
- 12:15 pm Snack
- 1:00 pm Retreat Ends

17

Practicing with Pain on Retreat

If mindfulness is to be relevant and liberating in all areas of our life, it needs to include discomfort. To be free only when we are comfortable is not the freedom Buddhism advocates: we find real freedom when we have inner peace and equanimity both in times of comfort and discomfort.

One area of discomfort experienced on retreat is physical pain; sooner or later, everyone who has a retreat practice will encounter pain in their body. While it may seem natural in daily life to avoid physical pain, experiencing it during retreats can be an important opportunity for practice. Rather than viewing pain as a problem, the first strategy is to see it as deserving careful attention, as an opportunity for investigation and personal growth. Mindfulness of pain can lead to Insight, peace, and inner freedom.

No retreat rule requires participants to endure pain. If changing our posture can alleviate pain, we are welcome to do so. However, when we see pain as a practice opportunity, it becomes interesting to allow it to remain, so that it can become the focus of mindfulness. How long we stay with the pain depends on how long we see this as a worthwhile opportunity, which will be different for everyone.

(People with a condition that brings unremitting pain should discuss this issue with a retreat teacher at the beginning of a retreat).

One practical reason to investigate pain is to learn if a physical issue needs to be addressed. In taking the time to feel and explore discomfort, we might learn what's causing it. For example, we may discover that the pain comes from tension in a part of our body. Relaxing the tension may lessen the pain. Pain may also arise when our posture is out of alignment. Investigating the pain may reveal that an adjustment in posture can reduce or alleviate the pain. It is then appropriate to shift the posture to one that might work better. In contrast, unconsidered changes to one's posture at the first signs of discomfort may temporarily ease the pain while shifting to another unbalanced posture causing a different discomfort soon enough.

Taking time to give careful attention to pain may help us recognize when it might be signaling the possibility of injury. Any time we suspect that an injury might occur we should adjust what we're doing. One warning sign of potentially injurious pain while in seated meditation is pain that persists for five minutes or more after getting up and moving. To avoid injury, we should find a different meditation posture that does not elicit the same pain.

When, on the other hand, pain carries no risk of injury, it can be helpful to explore it by letting it continue. Pain that's particularly useful to investigate is the discomfort that arises when chronically tense muscles—to which we've become insensitive or "numb" —begin to relax. With meditation, these areas begin to soften and wake up, and sometimes the first sensations that return are the pains of chronic tension. Patiently allowing the pain to continue may allow the muscles to further relax. Tense muscles in the shoulders and shoulder blade area often hurt as they relax; occasionally this is also the case in the chest or belly.

Pain may also arise when the meditation posture fatigues weak muscles that are engaged for long periods of time. For example, if we commonly sit hunched over, the back muscles required to sit up straight may quickly tire. When chronically tense muscles relax, we may need to engage previously under-used muscles to hold our posture. While overusing fatigued muscles is not helpful, it is also not beneficial to avoid the discomfort of tired muscles altogether. Using them enough—perhaps intermittently— is essential so they can gradually strengthen.

Mindfulness practice includes awareness of our reactions and beliefs about pain. Sometimes, rather than focusing on the pain, we can focus on our relationship to the discomfort. Are we impatient, aversive, angry, or afraid? Do we tense physically around the pain or contract mentally away from it? What beliefs do we have about pain? Are there unnecessary beliefs that magnify the pain or our impatience? Is pain seen as a personal failure or a shortcoming? Is it viewed as an obstacle? Sometimes these secondary reactions are more challenging than the bare, physical pain itself. They can also cause muscles around the pain to tense, thereby increasing the discomfort. By distinguishing our reactions from the primary physical sensations, we may find it much easier to be patient with pain and to decrease the tension around it.

Over time we can learn to have a more uncomplicated and easeful relationship with pain. We know how to experience it without creating stories about it. We may discover how to be aware without self-pity, fear, or resistance. Not only can we learn to be equanimous about pain, but we can also experience profound peace—even while pain is present. We can allow pain to be just pain, nothing more and nothing less, something that's simply occurring, without being a problem.

18

Practicing Mindfulness with Pain

Those times that you want to practice mindfulness of pain, it's helpful to use "the four foundations for mindfulness" as a guide. These "foundations" are four dimensions of our present-moment subjective experience that are effective for discovering the freedom that's possible with mindfulness. In relationship to pain, freedom means being aware of the pain without being caught up in it or resistant to it. Being mindful of pain in terms of how it appears for each of the four foundations—body, feeling tones, mind states, and mental processes—is an alternative to focusing on the thoughts and emotions flowing from our reactivity to the pain.

When pain is present, we can direct our awareness to register the associated physical sensations, feeling tones, mind states, and mental processes. The idea is not to use mindfulness as a technique to make the pain disappear. Rather, the approach allows attachments and distress to disappear. When this happens, the intensity of pain tends to lessen. And even if it doesn't, it could be an occasion to develop equanimity.

1. Mindfulness of the Body

The Buddha's instruction for the first foundation is to observe the body solely in terms of the body. Thus, we focus on the pain as a physical sensation independent of our emotional reactions or thoughts about those sensations. As if seeing the pain through a magnifying lens, we can direct attention to the specific area in the body where the pain occurs. As we bring mindfulness closer and closer to the direct experience of pain, it will sometimes transform into a kaleidoscopic dance of discrete sensations that arise and pass quickly. Occasionally the sense of pain will disappear, as all we are aware of are these rapidly changing sensations.

Because the word pain is an abstract concept, viewing it only through the lens of this word removes us somewhat from the direct experience. The label "pain" can quickly get us entangled in pain-related thoughts, memories, and expectations. Dropping the abstract concept of "pain" can make it easier to identify the specific physical sensations that make up the pain. Possible sensations include pulling, stabbing, tightening, burning, or aching. Some sensations, such as vibration and tingling, might be more neutral than unpleasant. The basic sensations may be easier to experience than our mental associations and fears about the pain.

2. Mindfulness of Feeling Tones

The second foundation of mindfulness is a step deeper into our subjective experience than the evident physical experience. Here we become aware of the feeling tone of the pain—i.e., the simple evaluation of its being either pleasant, unpleasant, or neutral. While pain is usually unpleasant to experience, it is not always so. When the shoulders are mildly painful their tension lessons, this pain can provide a mental pleasure if it is a sign that the shoulders are beginning to relax. Feeling a similarly mild ache may become very unpleasant if we believe it is the precursor of a severe illness.

By becoming aware of the feeling tone of the pain, it is possible to distinguish the feeling tone from any reactions and stories that arise. It may be easier to maintain a relaxed awareness of the simple experience of unpleasantness without further complications, such as negative interpretations or states of mind that strengthen the overall sense of unpleasantness. The mind can remain peaceful in the face of mild pain, and with mindfulness practice, this peace may be possible with even greater pain.

3. Mindfulness of Mind States

The third foundation of mindfulness takes us deeper into our subjective experience by focusing attention on our general state of mind or mood, often a more intimate and personal aspect of life than either our physical experience or the feeling tone of experience. The most straightforward approach to the third foundation is to be aware of whether our state of mind is tense or relaxed, contracted, or expansive. This approach can include recognizing if the overall condition of our mind is happy or sad, hostile, or kind, dissatisfied or content. Mind states often last longer than physical pain; therefore, the associated mood may persist when the pain has disappeared.

If we react to pain with negative mind states, we may further respond to the unpleasantness of the mental state itself so that it becomes the most challenging part of our experience of pain.

When physical sensations of pain, feeling tones, and mental states are all undifferentiated, it may be tricky to recognize the details of the experience. The whole experience may seem dense and impenetrable. Distinguishing these three parts can make it easier to be mindful of the particular mental activities that are considered part of the fourth foundation.

4. Mindfulness of Mental Processes

The fourth foundation is the most intimate aspect of our experience. It focuses on the mental activities that either bring us toward more suffering or happiness, to entanglement or freedom. This foundation is the heart of Dharma practice.

The simplest way of practicing this foundation is to recognize whether or not we are clinging to or resisting anything. When there is pain, do we meet it with craving, hostility, resistance, worry, or confusion? The fourth foundation includes discovering how mental suffering around pain comes from compulsively wanting things to be different. It also recognizes the corollary principle: mental freedom and peace come from letting go of this desire.

Ideally, practicing with pain on retreat is done with compassionate concern for ourselves. Being mindful of pain does not require stoicism, resignation, or duty. Instead, it is caring for ourselves through wisdom and reducing the inner roots of our suffering.

Because persistent pain on retreat can be tiring, it's essential to avoid spending too much time practicing with it. Spend some periods of meditation in a posture that is pain-free to refresh your mind and body. Pace yourself with pain, so you don't become grim or feel overwhelmed by it.

Retreats provide us with microcosms of how we react or respond in daily life. By studying our reactions to pain on retreat, we can become more knowledgeable about how we respond to challenges when we're not on retreat. We can learn not to get hooked on our reactions to pain. All of this teaches us lessons that are useful for the rest of our lives. Pain is a normal part of life. Becoming wise about it is one of the benefits of retreat practice.

19

Listening to Dharma Talks

The daily Dharma talk is an important part of Insight meditation retreats, especially if one listens with mindfulness, focus, and a clear idea of one's purpose for listening. Doing so can cultivate a receptivity that brings many benefits beyond the instruction, understanding, encouragement, or inspiration a talk may provide.

It was well known in ancient times that it's helpful to cultivate a receptive state of mind when listening to a Dharma talk. Texts describe the Buddha giving his most liberating teachings when his listeners were "ready, receptive, free from hindrances, uplifted and trusting." He understood this to be significant enough that he sometimes focused on getting the audience ready and receptive by first offering teachings that "inspired and gladdened" them.

To better experience the benefits of a Dharma talk, preparing for it is useful. Meditating shortly before a talk can calm any agitation or preoccupation that hinders listening. Being seated well before the talk begins gives us time to assume a posture conducive to listening, perhaps sitting in a way that is both comfortable and attentive. It allows time for the body to settle in, the mind to become quiet, and for us to assume an attitude of interest and receptivity.

Being receptive to hearing a talk is more than being ready and willing to listen; it is also a having willingness to learn something new and to be changed by what we hear.

Considering our intention and purpose for listening is also useful for becoming ready and receptive to a talk. If we know we have a strong tendency to listen for what we like or dislike, what we agree or disagree with, we might intentionally put this aside so we can learn something new. We might consciously correct for any passivity holding us back from engaging with the talk. Dharma talks are not events in which we settle back and let someone else entertain us. The receptivity of listening to a talk is participatory listening.

One participatory approach to listening focuses on learning the teachings taught. For this purpose, we may have a notebook to write down teachings that seem particularly useful to review later. Or we may listen attentively enough to remember some of the teachings, recognize the structure and logic of the talk, and actively reflect on what we hear.

Another approach is to allow the words to wash through us without lingering in thought about what we are hearing. This strategy works well if we listen with an open awareness, as if we were listening through the body. Trusting that our mind will take in and remember whatever might be important can facilitate listening to more than just the ideas.

Sometimes the teacher's quality of being while giving a talk can be more impactful than what they say. The teacher may convey a sense of calm, confidence, enthusiasm, compassion, or freedom that can be both inspiring and instructive. The manner of teaching may exemplify what is taught. When this is the case, we can focus on feeling, sensing, or attuning ourselves to the way the teacher teaches or to the quality of mind the teacher manifests.

Another option is to listen as a meditation practice focused on the words spoken and the voice speaking. Sometimes the tone, rhythm, and pace of a talk can help our mind become still, quiet, and concentrated. Some meditators find themselves more concentrated on listening to a talk than in any other circumstances, including meditation. Such concentration states can be particularly effective opportunities for certain teachings to penetrate deep in the mind, perhaps catalyzing significant Insight.

Among the many ways of listening to a talk, occasionally we can use a talk as a break from focusing on exhausting personal issues or meditation challenges. As a healthy distraction, the talk may provide rest, relaxation, and a reset that refreshes us to reengage with the meditation practice of the retreat.

Two primary factors help us decide what approach to take when listening to a Dharma talk. One factor is the purpose that the teacher has for giving the talk. The second is what is most suitable for ourselves and our practice at the time of the talk. Sometimes it is good to listen in a way that is receptive to the teacher's purpose. Other times it is best to listen in a way that supports the personal circumstances of our own practice and purposes. Ideally, we would find a way to match the purpose of the teacher with our own circumstances as a meditator.

Dharma teachers can teach with many different purposes in mind. Sometimes they intend to provide helpful instruction for a particular phase of the retreat. Sometimes a talk provides encouragement and inspiration for the practice. Other times, teachers explain the Dharmic context for the practice or offer perspectives on the many changing experiences, challenges, and joys of retreat practice. Teachers may tell stories that illustrate teachings and move us emotionally, so the teachings penetrate more deeply or help switch our moods to ones that are more supportive of our retreat practice. Occasionally, teachers may use a Dharma talk to model or transmit a way of being rather than imparting particular teachings. And sometimes, all these purposes can be present in a single Dharma talk.

If we can recognize the teacher's purpose, we then have the option to adjust ourselves accordingly. With instructions, we can focus on learning and remembering them. When practical teachings and perspectives are offered, we can reflect on when and how these may be useful. When a story is told, we might allow ourselves to be absorbed in the story. When we recognize that we can receive the most learning and inspiration from how a teacher is, we can turn our attention to hearing, observing, or feeling the teacher's quality of being more than what is spoken.

We can also consider our circumstances in deciding how to listen to a talk. If we need instruction, encouragement, inspiration, or new perspectives, we can listen attentively to a talk's content. If our meditation practice has a lot of momentum or some personal challenge is unfolding in significant ways, we may continue with our practice without paying attention to the content. If we are getting concentrated on listening to the talk, we might give ourselves over to this concentrated listening, allowing the mind to get more and more settled and calm. If the personal qualities of the teacher are meaningful, we can let this register deeply.

Over time, people who go on retreats will learn various ways of listening to Dharma talks. The more approaches to listening we cultivate, the more we can benefit from the many dimensions of Dharma talks. When we engage in the practice of listening to Dharma talks, we join the millions of people for whom, for 2500 years, the primary contact with Buddhism has been through listening to such talks. Our sincere wish to live a good life can build on the sincerity of the many people whose listening has kept the teachings alive since the time of the Buddha.

20

Mindfulness During Meals

On retreat, "mealtime is meditation time." This little slogan speaks to the great value of practicing mindfulness during meals. Mindfulness enhances food's emotional and psychological nourishment, and eating can be a significant activity for developing mindfulness. Mindfulness of our desires, beliefs, and reactions before, during, and after meals can reveal areas in which the path of freedom can open further. Careful attention to eating can also help us regulate our food intake so that overeating or undereating doesn't hinder our meditation practice. And when we wait in line and eat together with others, mealtime can be a time to experience the benefits and challenges of practicing in community.

Using mealtime to continue developing thoroughgoing mindfulness can be a powerful support for our retreat practice. The physical activity of eating can provide an engaging focus for staying mindful and concentrated. Mindfulness can be detailed as we remain attentive to picking up the fork, putting food on it, bringing the food into the mouth, chewing, swallowing, and then picking up the next forkful. Some people find it easier to maintain undistracted mindfulness while eating than during sitting meditation. Eating mindfully in the calm and silence of a retreat can be an occasion for a heightened enjoyment of meals that encourages continuity of mindfulness. The activity of eating and mindfulness can become mutually supportive joys.

Our relationship with food and eating is seldom simple. Retreats are an effective environment to become better aware of this relationship. In addition to noticing the act of eating, the silence and slowness of retreat life create opportunities to see desires, emotions, and beliefs that operate at mealtime. What are we thinking as we serve ourselves from the buffet line? What tensions or concerns appear at mealtimes? Are there multiple, perhaps conflicting, motivations around eating? Which motivations motivate us? How do we respond when a meal does not meet our preferences? Can we learn something about ourselves from the amount of food we put on our plates – is it too much or not enough?

Meal mindfulness includes our thoughts and feelings before and after eating. We may start thinking about an upcoming meal well before the mealtime itself. What thoughts, feelings, and concerns fuel this thinking? After a meal, do we judge ourselves for overeating or eating the wrong food? What motivates us to take our eating so personally that we get upset with ourselves? What beliefs do we have about how we eat? What ideas bring stress and lead to self-condemnation?

The following time-honored Buddhist practices associated with food can support investigating these questions and greatly enhance retreat practice. They can also be effective ways to get the most out of mindfulness of eating. Discovering how to be free regarding food, eating, and all that happens around meals is a valuable area of the Buddhist path.

Accepting What Is Given

First, we can practice "accepting what is given." This means eating the food that's offered unless there is a health reason not to do so. Limiting oneself to the food provided simplifies eating by putting preferences and desires aside. We can also learn about the ease that can come when we are not preoccupied with food choices. We simply eat what is offered and learn how to be content. Not acting on strong preferences and desires highlights them so we can study them. That can give us a chance to better notice our beliefs and fears surrounding food and eating. We can learn how strongly we hold ideas around what we need to eat or not eat, about what we want and don't want. These understandings can significantly support our practice of becoming free.

Eating what is offered can include putting aside efforts to optimize one's diet. It may not matter too much for the days of the retreat if we don't get our exact nutritional preferences met. By not focusing on nutritional optimization, a person may discover a more relaxed attitude around food, which can be a respite in light of the many media messages we receive. Inner peace is a nutrient at least as important as food.

Eating to Support Meditation Practice

The second Buddhist practice of eating is to "not eat for entertainment, distraction, pleasure-seeking or conceit." Instead, eat to maintain and nourish the body to support the meditation practice on retreat. Don't eat too much or too little. Notice when hunger has been satisfied and consider eating only a few bites more. Limiting oneself this way may reveal the many desires and impulses that keep us eating long after hunger has passed. One useful practice to do before taking a second helping is to consider our motivation for having more.

Mindfulness of the Body

The third helpful practice on retreat is to be mindful of the body while eating. When sitting down to eat, take the time to get centered in your chair and your body. As you eat, stay aware of the many bodily sensations that come into play. Be mindful of what happens in your mouth as you chew. What happens in your throat and stomach when you swallow? After you have put a bite of food in your mouth, wait to fill your fork or spoon until you have chewed and swallowed. Periodically pause in your eating to explore the shifts in sensations and feelings found in the body.

Mindfulness of the body while eating leads to better choices. We can notice when we are full and so become less likely to overeat. We may also become sensitive to the subtle physical signals about what to eat—e.g., more protein, fruit, or vegetables.

During retreats, mindfulness at mealtime includes more than attention to food and eating. Because we are eating in the company of others, mealtime can be a time to notice our relationships with other retreatants. Do we have a heightened concern about others during meals? Do we watch and judge others for what or how they eat? Are we worried that others are watching and judging us? Do we avoid others by coming late to meals and eating apart from others?

Sometimes people benefit from using mealtime as a break from the meditation schedule of a retreat, which can be wise if it provides needed relaxation or rest.

Approaching meals in this way can relieve tensions that may occur with the ongoing sitting and walking meditation schedule, and allow us to feel refreshed for the next meditation session. Relaxing and enjoying the meal can be a time to appreciate the gift of the food, the work of many people in the food preparation and cleanup, and being part of a community with fellow practitioners.

Practicing in Community

When we are part of a line of people at the serving table, we can learn to support the community by having relaxed, friendly attention to others who are also serving themselves food. We can give a bit of space to the people in front of us so they don't feel crowded or rushed. When a dish is running low, we can consider how much food to take so those after us can have some. Aware of the next person in line, we can return the serving utensil to a position where it is easiest for them to pick it up.

People new to retreats may find the silence during mealtime disconcerting. In ordinary life, if we sit at a table with other people and they are silent, don't acknowledge our arrival, and continue to look down at their food, this is likely unfriendly. It can take a few meals on one's first silent meditation retreat to realize that fellow retreatants are not being cold. Instead, as recommended, they are simply dedicated to staying mindful of their eating without being pulled into social interactions. After a few days, new retreatants generally not only become comfortable with the silence and lack of social interaction at meals, they also come to appreciate the relaxed way of being together with others that retreat meals provide.

Over time, bringing mindfulness to all aspects of mealtime, including our underlying beliefs, can lead to greater and greater ease around food. We can learn to simplify our desires around food so that eating can become a simple pleasure that's harmonious with a settled, peaceful mind, rather than a source of either excitement or agitation. We can learn how a healthy, mindful attitude around food can be an essential component of the path to freedom.

21

Practicing with Sleep

Meditation retreats are opportunities to bring mind-fulness to all aspects of our daily routines, including sleep. As a large part of every 24 hours is spent sleeping, retreat practice includes being mindful and intentional about our sleep. This is particularly relevant because people's sleep patterns and needs often change in retreat settings. With these changes, our relationship with sleep may shift as well. Approached with mindfulness and wisdom, our relationship with sleep can be an important arena for discovering freedom.

First Days—Settling In

It's common to be tired on the first day or so of a retreat. Sometimes this is because retreat participants have not had enough sleep in their daily lives. Sometimes it is because preparing for and traveling to the retreat can be taxing, especially if it means being busier than usual in the days preceding the retreat. For these reasons, it is wise to recognize first-day tiredness as just first-day tiredness without being angry, frustrated, or discouraged. Sleeping extra may be appropriate on the first day—e.g., by taking a nap. When the wake-up bell rings the first morning, sleeping longer is fine if needed.

Occasionally people do not sleep well the first night or two on retreat. There are many reasons for this. It can be from uneasiness due to being with many strangers, or it can be from sleeping in a new place. Sometimes it can be from enthusiasm or nervousness about being on retreat. If anxiety is the cause of sleeplessness, it can be helpful to do calming and reassuring activities before going to bed. If anxiety persists, try to be equanimous; being anxious about anxiety is not helpful.

Remembering that retreats are among the safest places to be can calm anxiety. Fellow retreatants are committed to kindness, goodwill, and harmlessness.

Changing Sleep Patterns

Many people find their sleep patterns differ when they're on retreat than when they're at home. Some people sleep more deeply; others sleep more lightly. Some will dream more vividly; others dream less – perhaps with no memory of dreaming. Some retreatants will discover they need more sleep, while others will need less. "Morning people" may find they do very well getting up to meditate before the wake-up bell and then going to bed before the last evening sitting. "Evening people" may prefer to stay up late, practicing well beyond the last scheduled meditation of the day.

Given the many individual variations in sleep, it is best

to avoid having a fixed idea about one's own sleep on retreat. Retreats are a good place to experiment with sleep. Some people will learn that too much sleep causes grogginess. Too long a gap between our last evening meditation and the first meditation the following day may interrupt the momentum of the practice. Too little sleep may give us less energy to practice throughout the day. As we learn from these experiments, we can adjust accordingly in subsequent days.

Sometimes more sleep is needed on retreats than at home. This may be particularly true when important psychological, emotional, and interpersonal issues become part of the retreat experience. If these experiences are exhausting, sleep may provide both needed rest and a chance for subconscious processing or sorting.

Some participants discover that their need for sleep decreases on one week or longer retreats. This may be because retreat life is simpler and less taxing than their daily life. It may be that meditation provides a deep rest that substitutes for sleep. Sometimes strong states of concentration are energizing enough to allow for less sleep.

Working Mindfully with Sleep and Dreams

Going to sleep and waking up are important times for mindfulness. These are times when many people do not practice mindfulness, giving in to old attitudes and thought patterns instead. However, it can be very supportive to our practice to be mindful just before falling asleep and when we're first waking up. The moments before falling asleep can be a time to check in with ourselves and take stock of how we are. We can also bring to mind something to contribute to an inspired and contented state of mind. Doing a few minutes of loving-kindness meditation while lying in bed can help lead us into deeper sleep.

How we fall asleep may also affect how we wake up. Spending a few minutes meditating before going to sleep may make it more likely that we begin to be mindful as we wake up. Similarly, when waking up in the morning, spending even a few minutes meditating while still lying down or sitting up in bed can create a good foundation for meditation throughout the day.

When dreams are significant enough to warrant attention, the approach on mindfulness retreats is to bring mindfulness to the emotions and body sensations that linger after the dream, rather than analyzing the content of the dreams. Just as we avoid stories and interpretations of what is happening while we meditate, while on retreat we avoid getting involved with the content of our dreams. What we can do, however, is bring attention to the lingering impact the dream has on our body, thoughts, and heart. In Insight meditation, the "royal road to the unconscious" is through the body, so practicing mindfulness of the body with the emotions that remain from a dream is helpful.

Persistent Sleepiness

Even if we have sufficient sleep, there are many reasons for tiredness during meditation retreats, each with its own antidote. Tiredness during the day may signify sinking into calmness or complacency. While calmness is usually helpful, it must be balanced with the appropriate effort. Therefore, applying more physical or mental effort can be useful when tired. This could be sitting up straighter or doing walking meditation, or even fast walking. Other times tiredness is a product of boredom, discouragement, or resistance. In such cases, patient perseverance and investigation of these states can be helpful. If emotional overwhelm is the reason for tiredness, it is sometimes best to take a break and do something comforting, such as a walk outside, observing a natural setting, or having a cup of tea.

Some people find it helpful to have a short nap every day during a retreat. The usual advice is to keep such naps short. The longer the nap, the more we interrupt the continuity and momentum of our meditation practice. Those who like to nap should experiment with one ten to fifteen-minute nap per day. This may be long enough to rejuvenate while maintaining the benefits of continuity of practice.

It is important to learn to practice mindfulness with tiredness and sleepiness and to develop the skill to keep meditating despite being tired. It can be beneficial to learn not to struggle while at the same time continuing with the meditation practice the best we can. Times of dullness, lethargy, lack of focus, and the drifting mind associated with drowsiness can strengthen equanimity and the capacity to start over with mindfulness repeatedly— maybe every few seconds. Sometimes a bit of sleepiness can even be helpful for meditation when less energy is available for being distracted.

Because sleep is an aspect of the retreat, it can be important to tell a retreat teacher about your sleep, especially if your sleep patterns or experiences change significantly from your usual routine. It is also helpful to discuss any persistent tiredness during the retreat with a teacher.

A meditation retreat is meant to be a safe, meaningful, and supportive environment to engage in practice and a path of meditation, liberation, and compassion. Hopefully, it is also a supportive environment to sleep deeply and contentedly.

22

The Practice of Work Meditation

At the Insight Retreat Center, short work periods are integral to our meditation retreats. They help create the balance between inner and outer mindfulness, between personal practice and practicing in community, and between stillness and activity. Learning that including work within the path of mindfulness practice can be one of the inspiring aspects of retreats.

Typically, at IRC, retreatants participate in two work periods each day: a simple 20-minute task just before breakfast, called "sangha (community) service," and a 40-minute period at some point later in the day called "work meditation." These work periods are done in silence except for brief exchanges needed to accomplish some tasks.

The morning period of "sangha service" is a time when all the retreatants work together to do the basic cleaning that cares for the center and the participants. It includes tasks such as sweeping the deck, mopping a hallway, cleaning bathroom sinks, dusting, etc.

The "work meditation" jobs are everyday tasks needed to operate a retreat. Many of these jobs are done in small teams. Examples include preparing food for a meal, washing dishes or pots, and doing kitchen laundry. The jobs are assigned with care so that the work is appropriate for each person.

The terms "sangha service" and "work meditation" convey the importance of these activities. Two meanings of the word service are implied when we refer to sangha service. Primarily it means an act of generosity in which one is serving the other participants of the retreat. By doing a simple daily task, each retreatant contributes to the well-being and comfort of the other retreatants. A second meaning refers to the sense of service as a ceremony or religiously significant act. Mindful cleaning can function as a kind of "ritual" affirmation and a reminder that Buddhist values can be found in our most mundane tasks.

The term "work meditation" indicates that this work period is just as important a time for mindfulness practice as the sitting and walking meditation. The point is not to rush through the task so one can have more time for "meditation" but to use it as an opportunity to practice mindfulness in action. It is a time to observe and let go of the many attitudes, beliefs, and feelings that interfere with having a meaningful awareness of the task, no matter what that task might be.

IRC retreats are entirely run by those practicing and training at the retreat. There is no staff apart from the practitioners. Retreatants form a mutually supportive community where everyone contributes their labor to help create the retreat environment. This mutual support becomes palpable and can be very nourishing. Working in this way emphasizes the important messages that we are all practicing together and that Buddhist practice includes caring for others and the place in which one practices.

An essential aspect of working on retreat is learning to be mindful, calm, and focused on the activity. Just like sitting and walking meditation, work meditation is a practice of repeatedly bringing our attention back to the present moment. In this way, it provides training much like the conventional meditation forms of sitting and walking.

Mindfulness of work includes becoming aware of how one engages in the work. For example, some people rush through their work because they believe it is vital to finish as quickly as possible. Others take too long because they are overly absorbed in the work. Both rushing and going slowly occur when we're not engaging in the task with an alert, mindful presence.

Our mind is the same whether we're engaged in sitting meditation or in work meditation. Just as the mind will wander off in thought during sitting meditation, it can also wander while working. Just as the five hindrances can "hinder" us while seated in the meditation hall, desire, aversion, dullness and weariness, restlessness and agitation, and doubt can hinder mindfulness and concentration when we're doing a job. Just as we can overcome a wandering mind and the hindrances when we're in seated meditation, we can with these forces in work meditation. When one focuses on work tasks on retreat, the mind can become concentrated, calm, and energetically balanced. It is also possible to have deep Insights.

On retreat, we can notice our attitudes toward work that can go unnoticed in ordinary life. A common discovery is the degree of self-consciousness we bring to a task—e.g., comparing ourselves to others, being concerned with what others think, doing the job to prove ourselves, or feeling inadequate. Retreats are a safe place to experiment with letting go of such self-concern so we can learn the pleasure of simple, direct focus on the task at hand.

Because work is a physical activity in which we're using our body, work meditation helps to foster greater mindfulness of the body. Our work tasks give us a rich opportunity to let go of mental preoccupations so we can pay attention to our body and how we engage the body in activity. Becoming more centered in the body through work greatly supports sitting meditation, helping mindfulness become "bodyfulness."

We get the most benefit from mindfulness when our meditation practice is part of a broader approach to spiritual growth that includes all aspects of our life. Mindful work helps create this breadth. By including work as part of a retreat, we can learn that mindfulness, peace, and spiritual freedom are not just found in meditation but also in the activities of daily life. If they are found only in meditation, one's freedom and peace have yet to fully mature. Work meditation is a training that can help with this maturation.

23

Practice Discussions on Retreat

Going on an Insight meditation retreat is like traveling with a guide into an unknown territory. On a retreat, the guides are the teachers, and the unknown territory is the depth of one's own heart and mind. A teacher guides in many ways—through instruction, teachings, exemplifying the practice, and individual discussions with retreatants.

Participants meet with the teachers during most retreats to discuss their retreat practice. Called "practice discussions" or "interviews," they provide practitioners with opportunities to explore themselves, the Dharma, and where these two meet. They are also occasions when retreatants can receive instruction and teachings specific to their circumstances.

Individual meetings with teachers are usually for fifteen minutes; a lot can happen in that short time if the conversation is focused, and explanations are honed to what is essential. If students are succinct, the teacher has more time to respond, offering thoughts and suggestions. Some people find it helpful to prepare for the meetings by writing down the main points they want to address.

If more than one teacher is leading a retreat, retreatants will normally have meetings with two of the teachers over the course of the retreat, alternating between them. There are a couple of reasons for this. First, meeting with different teachers allows retreatants to benefit from more than one perspective and approach. While all teachers deeply understand the Dharma, each one's style and personality are unique. In addition, meeting with different teachers allows participants to focus more on developing their meditation practice and personal relationship with the Dharma rather than on their relationship with a particular teacher.

Many factors influence the discussions between teachers and retreatants, and there's no "set way" for these meetings to go. While the primary purpose of these conversations is to support people's meditation practice, a wide range of topics may be discussed. For example, discussions might focus on clarifying the instructions or teachings. Or practitioners might report particular meditation experiences and challenges, or they may want to explore personal life issues through the perspective of mindfulness practice.

In most cases, retreatants initiate the topic for these discussions. Teachers will respond in various ways, depending on their teaching styles, the kind of practice taught on the retreat, and their best judgment about what would be most helpful. Depending on what the student presents, the teacher might listen deeply, offer understanding and encouragement, or ask questions. Sometimes they probe into the issue raised, give instruction and guidance, and challenge or affirm the practitioner's understanding.

Sometimes these meetings with teachers stir up anticipatory thinking, feelings, or anxiety. I've had people tell me they spent hours thinking about their interview. These thoughts and feelings are an integral part of one's Dharma practice. Rather than considering them distractions from meditation, they can be treated respectfully as something worthy of mindfulness. These are areas of the inner life where we can discover freedom and peace. It can be helpful to tell the teacher when there is a lot of thinking, planning, and anxiety before the meeting. The teacher may acknowledge the information and let the conversation move on to something else or choose to stay with the issue for further discussion or guidance. By bringing mindfulness to their relationship with a teacher, practitioners can learn how to practice with other relationships.

Now and then, a teacher will give instructions for how to do practice discussions. If no instructions are provided, retreatants are free to bring up any topic they think will support their meditation practice or any issue they wish to explore from a Dharma perspective. A meditation retreat is usually not the time for abstract discussions about the Dharma or long explanations of past events. Because the very purpose of retreats is to deepen one's practice, it's much more helpful to discuss topics that directly relate to one's practice and life.

So, what do people talk about in these interviews? Sometimes they ask questions about their meditation experience, the instructions, or the teachings. If they don't have questions, they might simply report how the practice is going. This report can include a brief description of their meditation approach and their intention for their practice. Even if practitioners follow meditation instructions given by the teacher, when they explain the practice in their own words, the teacher can then offer input and refine the instruction. These reports can also include an account of what the person finds challenging and what is going well. If a practitioner notices that one's reports always focus on challenges—or the opposite, on what is going well—it can be helpful to consider what is left out.

Sometimes meetings with teachers focus entirely on what is happening in the present moment during the practice discussion itself. This can be a mindful exploration of the student's experience at the moment, in the meeting.

Similar to how practitioners stay attentive to present-moment experiences in meditation, they can also do this during the discussion with the teacher. The teacher might ask questions or guide this exploration. The willingness to be honestly open about one's present-moment experience in the presence of a teacher can help a practitioner develop a profound trust in the potential of mindfulness.

Occasionally a person's meditation unfolds so that very little is said during these meetings. This might happen when mindfulness, concentration, and inner freedom are strong enough to evoke a profound peace where nothing needs to be discussed, and nothing needs to happen. Instead, the practitioners stay in touch with their inner stillness and let whatever is spoken emerge out of that peace. If nothing is said, the internal state communicates for itself. When appropriate, the teacher's inner freedom may meet the practitioner's state.

The role of a teacher on retreat is to serve and support the practice and awakening of everyone participating in the retreat. Practicing on retreat is one of the most noble and sacred things a person can do. For teachers, meeting with those who do this practice, whether they are new to retreats or experienced, is a great honor.

24

Mindfulness of Attitude

The English word *attitude* comes from the 17th-century French word of the same spelling, referring to how someone was positioned in a work of art. Given its capacity for great beauty, the mind might be seen as a work of art—perhaps as a kind of painting. The attitudes we have determine the composition of this painting. Some attitudes contribute to its beauty, while others detract from it. The Buddha taught that it is possible to "adorn the mind" (*cittalankara*), and that the mind can be radiant like pure gold, provided it is purified, just as gold is purified of its dross.

Mindfulness of our attitude is at the heart of meditation practice. We can think of our attitude as the soil in which meditation develops and the heart and mind transformed. Nothing useful can grow if the soil is infertile, dry, or impenetrably hard. Plant growth will be stunted if toxins seep through the soil. If, on the other hand, the soil is soft and moist with humus, wonderous life of all kinds can flourish.

But just what do we mean when we refer to our "attitude"? Our attitude is the manner in which we feel, think, and respond to our experiences. It can operate as a filter that can greatly influence what we do, say, or think. An attitude may be situation-specific, or it can be an ongoing disposition controlling how we respond to circumstances. Attitudes may be short-lived or persist for years and decades. When they continue for a long time, they shape our temperament. When deeply engrained, they may seem so normal they become invisible to us.

A critical function of mindfulness meditation is to discover the attitudes we bring to meditation. Because many of our everyday attitudes can be more counterproductive while meditating than in daily life, meditation is a valuable arena to notice unhelpful attitudes. Any time we believe meditation is not going well is the right time to consider whether our attitude is the real issue that needs to be addressed.

If our debilitating attitudes go unrecognized, they can fester and create tension. An attitude may cause only mild anxiety or stress at any given moment, but if it is chronically reinforced, the distress and suffering can become great. Becoming aware of debilitating attitudes is the first step to becoming free of them.

Some common attitudes that hinder meditation are ambition, striving, having expectations, needing control, and impatience with challenges. Attitudes about oneself that are not helpful are conceit, lack of confidence, self-criticalness, self-indulgence, self-deprecation, and self–preoccupation. Also unhelpful is to be aversive toward any of these unhelpful attitudes.

Unhelpful attitudes from daily life that may be carried into meditation include aversion, anxiety, drives for comfort and pleasure, chronic analyzing, fear of failure, holding ourselves to high standards of success, and needing to prove ourselves.

When any of these or other hindering attitudes occur in meditation, it's all too easy to be pulled so strongly into the world of thinking (and perhaps criticizing) that we spend very little time meditating. These attitudes can contribute enough agitation to interrupt the continuity of mindfulness and to prevent the mind from settling. Even more challenging can be the sense of frustration they may evoke.

If we only learn a particular meditation technique without learning the basic attitudes that are supportive of meditation, our habitual attitudes can then easily persist and, without our knowing, undermine our practice. But if we learn helpful attitudes for practice, we can apply them when we meditate.

Many different attitudes can support us in our meditation practice. Some are appropriate for particular circumstances or particular phases of practice. Some are antidotes or medicine for the attitudes that undermine us. Once we become familiar with the attitudes that hinder our practice, we will, over time, acquire a growing knowledge of the useful attitudes.

Here are examples of basic attitudes that are conducive to mindfulness meditation:

- It is enough to recognize what is happening; nothing needs to be fixed or changed.
- Have patience with all that happens; being in a hurry is a form of greed.
- There is nothing to prove or resist in meditation; use it to learn something new about being peaceful.
- Your capacity for attention is a treasure.
- No message that you are less than beautiful is worth believing.
- Trust the awareness that flows out of stillness.

The common element in these six attitudes is that they promote calm, non-reactive attention (including calm, non-reactive attention to our reactivity). They do not involve trying to change what is happening; they are part of finding a useful, meditative way of being aware of what is happening.

Other, more active attitudes may also be helpful to cultivate. An attitude of kindness, compassion, and letting go can be beneficial. Tapping into the confidence from whatever faith or trust we have in practice is another useful mindset. So too is a sense of blamelessness that comes with living a life of ethical integrity. Not only do these attitudes function as antidotes to their opposites, but they are also nourishing in and of themselves. Nourishing ourselves with skillful attitudes is a vital pleasure of meditation.

As meditation develops, each person will learn which attitudes are most useful. Often, we discover that what is helpful at one phase of practice is no longer useful later. Sometimes a firm, unwavering commitment is beneficial; other times, a soft, relaxed attention that allows things to unfold on their own is most helpful. When developing our mindfulness, different attitudes may be more useful than when cultivating concentration. For example, it is helpful to avoid believing there are such things as distractions when doing mindfulness meditation; instead, these are considered appropriate subjects to hold in awareness. In doing concentration practice, on the other hand, it might be helpful to recognize distractions as something to be let go of or to ignore in favor of more fully focusing on the object of concentration.

One way of being mindful of our attitudes is to distinguish between what is happening and our relationship to what is happening. Seeing this distinction can create space or a pause between the two. This space is a doorway to peace. Seeing the difference between what is happening and our relationship to it also allows us to consider whether the attitude embedded in the relationship is skillful.

Liberation brings a shift in the relationship we have with experience. This relationship is freed from craving, clinging, and attachments. The attitudes that support the path of liberation are those that share in some qualities of liberation itself. For example, an attitude of equanimity shares some of the non-reactivity that becomes complete in liberation. An attitude that inclines toward letting go of clinging matures into the full letting release of the mind's liberation. An attitude of non-contention or non-conflict with whatever happens in meditation is a foretaste of the peace of liberation. In these ways, we find that attention to our attitude is central to meditation practice and the path of liberation.

If meditation is the art of beautifying the mind, attending to our attitudes is key to this beautification. This includes being kind, patient, equanimous, and without conflict, as we attend to our attitudes. There is no path to freedom without traces of the goal in the path itself.

25

Cultivating Compassion

Compassion is an invaluable companion on a multiday residential Insight retreat journey. Compassion can be the motivation for this practice as well as a result. As our inner freedom grows, our capacity for compassion increases; as our compassion increases, so does the importance of freedom from suffering. Liberation supports compassion, and compassion supports liberation—both benefit when they go hand in hand.

Compassion is a form of empathy and care that wishes to alleviate someone's suffering. Known as karuna in Buddhism, this compassion is sometimes referred to as the "jewel in the lotus." The lotus symbolizes the heart or mind that, with practice, blossoms into freedom, and the jewel represents the compassion appearing in the center of this blossom. The feeling of unfettered compassion is one of the most beautiful feelings a person can experience, providing valuable meaning and purpose to any human life. Buddhism celebrates its presence as an inner wealth and source of happiness.

Given its importance, Buddhism doesn't leave the manifestation of compassion to chance. We don't have to passively accept how often and how strongly we happen to experience it. Instead, we can develop our compassion and remove the obstacles that stand in its way.

Because people sometimes confuse compassion with feelings of distress, it is helpful to distinguish these two clearly. Compassion doesn't make us victims of suffering, whereas feeling distress does. Learning how to see the suffering in the world without taking it personally is very important; taking it personally is to become depressed or burdened by assuming inappropriate blame and responsibility for someone's suffering. We can avoid this if we learn to feel empathy without mixing it with our fears, attachments, and perhaps unresolved grief.

We need to understand our suffering to feel greater compassion for others. Mindfulness practice is a great help in this. With mindfulness, we can better see our suffering, its roots within us, and the way to freedom from suffering; we can begin to cultivate both equanimity toward our suffering and release from its causes.

In this regard, it's helpful to appreciate the great value of staying present, open, and mindful of suffering, both our own and that of others. We often need time to process difficult events and experiences and let difficult emotions move through us. When immediate action is not required, staying mindful of suffering doesn't necessarily require a lot of wisdom or special techniques. It mostly takes patience and perseverance. Relaxed mindfulness of our suffering increases our ability to feel empathy for others' difficulties and pain. It gives time for understanding and letting go to occur. By practicing mindfulness of habitual reactivity, we can take the time to see and feel more deeply what is happening. This allows empathy to grow and more profound responses to arise. In this way, compassion may be awakened rather than intentionally created.

Some people are reluctant to actively cultivate compassion because they worry it will be insincerely or artificially contrived. Others fear that it will make them sentimentally naive or prevent them from seeing others clearly or realistically—perhaps out of worry that they will be taken advantage of if they are compassionate to others. While there may be some wisdom in these concerns, only by taking some risks in having compassion can we learn wise compassion.

One effective way of developing compassion is creating conditions that make it more likely to occur. Rather than directly trying to make ourselves more compassionate, we can engage in activities that increase the likelihood that compassion will arise.

A condition for compassion is a sense of safety. It is easier to feel compassionate if we feel safe, and difficult when we don't. Therefore, finding appropriate ways to feel safe can be helpful. Locking ourselves in our homes may feel secure, but it's not conducive to caring more about others. Learning how to be safe while in the world is more valuable. So is using mindfulness practice to address some of the anxieties and self-preoccupations that make us more likely to feel threatened.

It's important, however, not to feel obligated to be compassionate, as this often leads to self-criticism and stress that interferes with the arising of true compassion. Buddhism doesn't require us to feel empathy and care for others. It does say, however, that we can be compassionate and that doing so is a wonderful asset to ourselves, others, and the practice of freedom. The focus can be on how compassion enriches us, not depletes us.

Some people hesitate to cultivate compassion because they worry they'll have to give up too much of themselves as they help others. Or they fear they will have to spend time with uncomfortable people. By knowing we are not obligated to be compassionate, it may be easier to use our best wisdom and common sense to understand when acting on compassion is appropriate and when it is not.

Having confidence in our skill to respond to others' suffering is another condition that can make it easier to feel compassion. If we feel helpless, too uncomfortable, or even threatened by the troubles others are facing, awareness of their suffering might add to a sense of personal threat. Developing our ability to be present and respond to suffering has a lot to do with slow and patient training in mindfulness, concentration, and letting go.

A practical way of strengthening compassion is to understand and then release whatever stands in its way. For example, tension and stress limit compassion. When we're stressed, we're usually too preoccupied for empathy to operate. When we're relaxed, however, our capacity for empathy increases. People who cultivate deep states of calm often find that it naturally opens their hearts to great abilities of compassion and love. Selfishness and self-preoccupation also obstruct compassion by blocking the attention and sensitivity that's needed for compassion to arise. One benefit of letting go of selfishness is that compassion arises more easily.

We can also increase the compassion we feel in our lives by setting the intention to do so. This intention can be specific, such as intending to be compassionate in a particular situation or toward a particular person—or it can be general, such as intending to practice compassion for a day or week. With such intentions, we're more likely to remember to focus on compassion and to recognize more compassionate thoughts and impulses as they occur.

Valuing compassion when it does appear can also strengthen it and make it more apt to arise in the future. We might consider and appreciate the benefits it can bring others and ourselves. Knowing that compassion can bring happiness may make it more appealing. Compassion for others can be a relief when we've spent a long time being preoccupied with ourselves.

Another supportive condition is to reflect deliberately on compassion, perhaps stimulated by regularly reading and talking to others about it. Whatever we think about regularly can become our inclination. If we repeatedly think about love, kindness, and caring for others, compassion-related thoughts are likely to appear more often.

Spending time with compassionate people can also help us. The people we frequently see often influence us. Seeing compassion in others can inspire it in us.

Finally, understanding that compassion is a form of love helps us recognize what a jewel it truly is. When it arises from inner freedom, it is then connected to other beautiful capacities of our hearts such as well-being, calm, clarity, and peace.

It turns out that there's a great deal we can do to make compassion a more central part of our lives. As compassion grows, our self-centeredness and clinging decrease. As these decrease, compassion becomes more readily available. To let compassion and liberation support each other is one of the most beautiful ways of training in the Buddhist path. It can be our gift to the world.

26

Dharma Service on Retreat

Many people are first motivated to participate in meditation retreats to deepen their meditation practice or address their personal suffering. At some point, this motivation can transform into a growing interest in supporting others to deepen their practice and overcome their suffering. At this point, we may begin to practice for the benefit of others, not just for ourselves. This expansion of our motivation is often a natural outgrowth of Buddhist practice, as self-preoccupation lessens and our capacity for empathy and generosity increases. Because they are intimately interrelated, the welfare of others becomes as important as our own welfare. The two can grow together in mutual support: as we benefit others, we benefit ourselves, and as we benefit ourselves, we benefit others. This is known as the "Dharma of mutual benefit."

Practicing for the benefit of others can take many forms. It can involve a dedication to mature further along the path of liberation so we become kinder, freer, wiser, and more generous. It can also take the form of actively supporting others in their practice. When this support is offered through our time and personal labor, it is called "Dharma service."

Dharma service is central to meditation retreats at the Insight Retreat Center. Every morning all retreatants participate in 20 minutes of "Sangha Service," where much of the basic cleaning of the center occurs. As the name implies, this cleaning is a way to serve the retreat community. It's through the Dharma service of volunteers that registration, cooking, managing, and many other significant operations of IRC retreats are accomplished. Those who do this work provide the opportunity for others to benefit from retreat practice. In addition, and perhaps more importantly, Dharma service infuses a retreat with goodness, generosity, and compassion that greatly support the deep inner work of meditation. It shows what is possible when self-centeredness and fear no longer dominate one's life

Dharma service is as much about serving fellow retreatants as it is about getting the work done. It is work imbued with the good intentions of those doing the work. Retreatants can often feel this goodness and may be inspired by it in their retreat practice. For those offering service, the work brings joy both in providing an outlet for their goodwill and care and in knowing that they're benefiting others. Offering Dharma service so others can engage in Dharma practice is one of the most rewarding activities of retreat life.

Sometimes Dharma service on retreats is inspired by the wish to offer something back for the benefits one has received. It is an expression of the saying, "Gratitude begets generosity." When expressed, gratitude has a chance to grow into its full potential as a nourishing and calming force.

Sometimes Dharma service becomes an opportunity to bring our practice to activities that are as valuable for spiritual growth as meditation. Indeed, the service work we do and the interpersonal contacts it entails provide a rich area for Dharma practice. While the work we do and the interactions the work involves may be similar to those that occur in daily life, because we're on retreat, we have a much greater ability to find the Dharma in the midst of Dharma service. The work can bring Insights about ourselves and about doorways to inner freedom. The personal and interpersonal challenges that may arise during service work can thus become nourishing food for practice. Through Dharma service, we may grow in ways that don't usually happen in meditation. When we offer Dharma service on retreat, it expands the practice potential of the retreat.

One benefit of engaging in forms of Dharma service that have added responsibilities is that they put us into more contact with the retreat teachers. Cooks, managers, and teachers may have regular conversations and meetings about work and retreat issues. In this way, these service leaders and the teachers get to know each other in broader ways than when one is an ordinary participant in a retreat. Teachers are inspired by the generosity and mindfulness they see in the cooks and managers. With more teacher contact, cooks and managers sometimes have unique opportunities to witness how teachers address issues that arise. There's a saying that "Teachers teach more by how they are than by what they say." Those doing Dharma service often have frequent opportunities to witness how teachers conduct themselves.

Just as we can practice meditation for an entire lifetime, so we can do the work of Dharma service when we bring as much mindfulness, ease, and liberating Insight to doing service as we do to formal meditation. And as meditation reveals greater dimensions of selflessness, Dharma service is also a wonderful arena to discover and express this dimension in the rest of our lives. Selfless Dharma service can expand far beyond retreats; it can become what we offer the world wherever we go and whatever we do. In its full maturation, Dharma service is life unfolding from the most profound and beautiful dimensions of our hearts.

27

Going for Refuge

Buddhist teachings often emphasize the goal of awakening. In practice, however, the inner transformation known as "going for refuge" can be almost as significant as awakening itself. "Going for refuge" refers to the decision to base our life on walking the path to liberation. When we go for refuge, we align ourselves with the goodness and truth arising from non-clinging.

Two related meanings of the English word refuge highlight the value of *sarana*, the Buddhist word for "refuge." The first meaning refers to a place where people can find safety from danger. The second meaning refers to an area, like a wildlife sanctuary, set up to protect and support what is considered valuable. In Buddhism, going for refuge includes both of these meanings: protecting ourselves from danger and safeguarding what is most valuable or beautiful within us.

The practice of going for refuge is as ancient as Buddhism itself. It began with those who, after meeting the newly awakened Buddha, were so moved they spontaneously declared their dedication to him and his teachings (i.e., the Dharma). They stated this dedication by saying they were "going for refuge" in the Buddha and the

Dharma. As some of his disciples also experienced awakening, they became the Sangha—the community of awakened people. Subsequently, people went for refuge to the "Three Jewels," i.e., the Buddha, Dharma, and Sangha.

Sometimes the Triple Refuge refers to the historical Buddha, the Dharma he taught, and the Sangha of practitioners who have followed in his footsteps over the centuries. They can be called the "external refuge" because they exist outside us. But the Triple Refuge also refers to inner qualities that give rise to the Buddha, the Dharma, and the Sangha. Since these are inner states or capacities that we all have, this can be called the "internal refuge."

The external refuge in the Buddha is important because few people readily discover on their own the full potential they have for spiritual transformation. It's helpful, therefore, to have the Buddha as an example of what is possible for each of us. The Dharma teachings provide instruction in practices that lead to awakening and protection from taking paths that lead away from it. The Sangha provides support from those who are familiar with the path of practice.

The internal refuge in the Buddha calls on and builds our inner capacities. It is the refuge obtained by recognizing and developing the peace of non-harming and nonattachment. It is a vision that affirms the possibility of uprooting the fear, hate, delusion, and greed that are the sources of our suffering. And it is the intuition that freedom is possible. To take inner refuge in the Buddha is to rely on deep confidence in our potential for spiritual growth and transformation.

The internal refuge in the Dharma takes different forms, all of which point to the value of Dharma practice. Because one of the primary characteristics of the Dharma is non-harming, one powerful way to rely on the inner refuge is to have a commitment to non-harming. The Dharma is not an abstract principle; rather, it arises from how we are and what we do. When we dedicate our lives to non-harming, the Dharma flows through our lives, allowing us to practice the Buddha's teachings.

The internal refuge in Sangha encompasses our capacity to have mutually supportive relationships for walking the path of liberation. Central to this is our goodness, kindness, compassion, and generosity toward others and ourselves. Walking the path of non-harming and awakening does not depend only on our efforts to practice; it is also supported by relationships with others that are characterized by wholesome feelings, motivations, and attitudes. We are all capable of these states but often overlook them. To take refuge in the inner Sangha is to have confidence in our inner goodness, even when it may not be readily apparent.

The inner Buddha, Dharma, and Sangha are what the Buddha referred to when he encouraged people to take refuge in themselves. In the last days of his life, he said, "You should live as your own refuge with no one else as your refuge. You should live with the Dharma as your refuge with no other refuge." The first sentence suggests that people must walk the path of practice for themselves; no one else can walk it for them. The second sentence indicates that the Dharma is found within us, in our own capacities.

Some people look to the Buddha, Dharma, and Sangha for refuge when the things they previously relied on no longer support them. Changes in our work situation, finances, relationships, health, and society can show us that these are unreliable for lasting happiness. Dharma practice reveals an inner source of contentment and satisfaction that is reliable. This source is represented by the Buddha, Dharma, and Sangha when we find them in our inner wisdom, peace, and non-contentious relationship with reality.

The Buddha, Dharma, and Sangha can sustain us in difficult times. They encompass values, practices, insights, and realizations that protect us from self-destructive behaviors and help us live wisely. They help bring forth the best qualities of heart.

When we go for refuge, we orient ourselves by what the Buddha, Dharma, and Sangha represent. This could be as simple as deciding, "From now on, I orient my life to being very careful with my speech so that it is honest." It could be the dedication, "I will try to live my life without harming others." For some, it may involve a radical, even revolutionary, change in how they live their lives as they dedicate themselves to liberation, wisdom, and compassion.

Some people approach going for refuge as a firm, courageous, and enthusiastic commitment to a life based on spiritual freedom and compassion. It is a commitment that simultaneously energizes us to act in new ways while encouraging deep relaxation. We can let go of many unnecessary things when we trust that the Dharma path provides meaningful and profound support. Going for refuge in the Buddha, Dharma, and Sangha protects us from danger as much as it nourishes the growth of what is most beautiful within us.

28

The Dana of Dana Retreats

At the Insight Meditation Center we offer all our programs at no cost. The same is true at the Insight Retreat Center, where our residential retreats are provided freely to anyone who participates. We do this because we believe Buddhist practice unfolds best in a field of generosity, gratitude, and goodwill. The freely given aspect of retreats exemplifies the remarkable inner freedom that Buddhism champions. By demonstrating an alternative to our culture's dominant materialism and greed, we hope these retreats inspire open-heartedness and open-handedness in the volunteers who put on the retreats, the donors who fund them, and the retreatants themselves.

When we offer a retreat, we consider it a gift to those attending. We use the Buddhist word dana, meaning "gift," when we describe our retreats as dana retreats. The other reason we use the word dana to refer to our retreats is that all the volunteer efforts that allow us to put on a retreat are also gifts. Dana Retreats are both gifts to the retreatants and gifts given by the people who make them possible.

The staff and teachers who run the retreat do so as volunteers providing the gift of their labor and time. Many people volunteer because they want others to experience the benefits retreats can provide. Because of all this volunteerism, retreatants often find themselves inspired, knowing they are being cared for by the non-obligatory generosity of others. It is a kind of inspiration through which the benefits of retreat can sink in deeper.

Generosity, gratitude, and goodwill thrive more easily when no pressure exists. We aspire, therefore, to operate our retreats and retreat center without financial stress. For the most part, we have managed this because we are blessed by the many people who have been supporting our efforts.

We are happy that offering retreats freely removes a financial obstacle for some people. It frees us at IRC from having to administer scholarships and eliminates, for many people, the awkwardness of asking for a scholarship. Instead of having special scholarship fundraising efforts that benefit only some people, all our fundraising efforts benefit everyone who comes to retreats.

Most of the financial support for our retreats and retreat teachers comes from the donations retreatants offer at the end of retreats. Retreatants are neither required to donate nor are there any dollar amounts suggested. But when they donate, their generosity allows others to participate in upcoming retreats. When people give knowing others will benefit, their giving can be a source of joy— their giving benefits the giver.

We could, of course, charge for our retreats. Not only is there nothing inherently wrong with this, but there is also some wisdom in doing so. However, try this thought experiment: what difference would it make to you if you paid a required cost for a retreat before the retreat versus freely offering the same amount of money as a donation at the end?

While the clarity of knowing a set cost can have advantages, it doesn't allow people to experience the joy of being generous. When people pay for something, there is often a belief that they deserve something in return, an attitude that can get in the way of the personal work meditation requires. Because people don't pay for our retreats, people are less likely to assign responsibility to others. Instead, people are more likely to feel gratitude that someone at a previous retreat offered the funds so they could attend their retreat. Gratitude, in turn, can help people relax and trust, qualities that support meditation practice and inspire people to do the inner work of meditation. Gratitude benefits the grateful.

Everything is Practice

It is a joy and privilege to support others in doing the deep inner work that can occur on retreats. Not only are we at IMC inspired to offer retreats, but we are also inspired by the goodwill and generosity of the many people who support our retreat efforts. It takes a community to support awakening in each one of us.

150

29

The Practice of Leaving a Retreat

The end of a meditation retreat is as important as any other part, and approaching it as a significant practice period can lead to many benefits. The last day of a retreat and the days following provide substantial opportunities for Insight and self-understanding. Instead of discontinuing the practice because calm, concentration, or mindfulness has decreased, it's helpful to end a retreat with the intention to process, absorb, and integrate the retreat experience. In this way, a retreat can have greater lasting value. The transition associated with leaving a retreat begins when our thoughts turn toward the ending and leaving the retreat center. Increased thinking and excitation usually mark this shift. Generally, the influence of the end begins about six-sevenths of the way through a retreat. For a seven-hour retreat, this may be an hour or so before the end. For a seven-day retreat, the transition may begin about a day before the end. For month-long retreats, it can begin as much as 3-4 days before the close. This way the length of the ending mirrors the length of the retreat points to the naturalness of the process.

Many people believe the important part of a retreat is attaining deeper experiences of concentration, calm, or clarity. When, near the end, they seem to be surfacing from whatever depth they've reached, it can be easy to conclude that the practice momentum is gone. Some people will then spend the last hours or days of the retreat just going through the motions, not seeing value in continuing to practice wholeheartedly. However, some of the most important Insights and realizations on a retreat can occur as we emerge from whatever stillness we've attained. Staying attentive and interested in what happens as we approach the end of the retreat increases the likelihood of experiencing these Insights and realizations.

At some point near the end, mental patterns that receded or fell away during the retreat often return. Everyday worries and desires, personal problems or challenges, and increased self-consciousness may all reappear. Because we are still on retreat, we can find a different vantage point from which to observe them. With more sustained mindfulness than is available in daily life, we can look more deeply at our mental tendencies or notice parts of our mental ecology that go unseen in the busyness of everyday life. It might be possible to shift the relationship to our feelings, emotions, and thoughts by viewing them with equanimity, acceptance, and kindness. It's possible to observe what the mind is doing instead of getting entangled with it. During this transition period, just as throughout a retreat, we can explore what we might be clinging to and how we might be able to let go. In fact, some forms of clinging are more easily discovered near the end of a retreat. Simply asking ourselves, "What am I clinging to?" may reveal attachments that underlie how the mind operates. We might discover what lies beneath our attachments by considering, "Why am I clinging to this?" These inquiries can be beneficial and yield Insights even though we may be less concentrated or still than earlier in the retreat.

It's helpful to consider the idea that a retreat actually lasts twice as long as its official length, and that when we leave a retreat, it's only half over. Thus, a one-week retreat continues for an additional week after its end; a month-long retreat continues for another month. During this "second half," we may still experience the effects of the retreat. There may be unaccustomed energy and mood shifts. Particularly on the day the retreat ends, some people become uncharacteristically energetic, perhaps talking quickly and lengthily. Some people become tired, with a desire to nap or be alone, and others become over-stimulated quickly. Sometimes even going into a supermarket can feel overwhelming. Occasionally people become easily irritated a day or two after a retreat because of the stark contrast between daily life and the calm and well-being of the retreat. Sometimes annoyance arises because all our emotions are flowing more freely.

Coming off retreat, we may not see or appreciate the full context of our life because we're still in retreat mode. For this reason, it's best to avoid making significant decisions or coming to grand conclusions about our life during this unofficial "second half of the retreat." Instead, it's helpful to spend ample quiet time during this period. Meditating, going for walks, and refraining from lots of email, TV, or computer time may allow deeper reflection about what is essential.

The post-retreat period is an excellent time to integrate or digest the retreat's benefits, learning, or inspirations. Living calmly and simply in the days after the retreat may let these stay current in our mind so they can continue to ripen. Rushing back to a fully packed life may cut short this ripening. Taking time for reflection, journaling, or talking with a trusted friend about the retreat may also deepen the lessons and benefits. Meditating two or three times a day in the days after a retreat can be very supportive of this integration process. Extra meditation can also help bring emotional and mental balance if one feels particularly sensitive after the retreat.

The entire meditation retreat is meant to be an integrated experience; the formal closing period is part of the retreat's overall process. If we leave before the closing talks, the breaking of silence, and the chance to say goodbye, we miss a significant opportunity and may leave part of what is "cooking" on retreat "half-baked." It can also shortchange the important interpersonal aspects of a retreat. Retreat practice is a collective practice where retreatants mutually support and benefit each other.

Finally, from the perspective of ongoing mindfulness practice, the "end" of a retreat is arbitrary. Bringing the practice into one's life includes practicing before, during, and after the retreat. The practice continues in whatever new circumstances we find ourselves. One of the great values of a mindfulness retreat is the way it develops greater confidence and inspiration in being mindful wherever we are. Leaving a retreat is just another circumstance in which to be mindful.

30

Skillful Evaluation of Meditation Practice, Part 1

After a person has been meditating for some time, it's helpful to evaluate how the practice is developing. Does it need adjustment or renewal? Is it the right practice to do? Such evaluations can be done alone or with a teacher.

Taking a step back to assess our meditation should be a manageable task. We are evaluators by nature, assessing and drawing conclusions all the time, even if subconsciously. We decide what clothes to wear after considering many factors, not least the weather. Going for a walk requires various considerations: How far will I walk? Do I need to prepare? If it's a long walk, do I need to pace myself? What is the best route, the best pair of shoes?

In the same way, we can evaluate our practice. It's best to do this in a balanced way: not too little or too much. We may assess too little because of complacency, excessive reliance on faith in the practice or teachings that downplay the role of intelligent reflection. At other times, we might over-evaluate and tie ourselves up in knots.

Over-evaluating can undermine our progress, like the farmer pulling out a corn seedling to see if it's growing. Imagine trying to learn to ride a bike while obsessively asking ourselves, "Am I doing this right? How do I look?"

Sometimes we're looking for approval when we should be looking for balance. Sometimes we expect perfection when what is needed is patience and persistence.

Below is a list of areas for evaluating your practice. While no two practitioners are alike, these are general areas to check that can give you a good idea of where you are.

Motivation

First, ask yourself what your motivation is. Why are you practicing? Meditation practice flourishes when supported by clear intention. There are many answers to this question. Because no one else should decide your goals, it is helpful to reflect on this. I regularly advise people to discover what their deepest intention is. What do they most want? What is their heart's deepest wish? Our practice can have the most value when connected to what is most important to us.

Our intention may be well-understood, or it may be obscure. Chances are you've experienced both of these states. Sometimes, early on, I intuitively knew I wanted to meditate, but I didn't know why. I just knew there was a strong pull toward practice. At other times, the reason was clear: I knew I suffered and wanted to be free of my suffering. Sometimes I was aware of conventional suffering; sometimes, although free of conventional suffering, I had a clear Insight that there was a deep, inner dissatisfaction at the core of my mind. I wanted to find, touch, and understand this core. Meditation was the only route I knew to reach this core, and I was highly motivated to do so.

Our motivation can be to cultivate beautiful qualities of the heart and mind—love, peace, courage, compassion, Insight, understanding, the pursuit of the truth, and liberation. Developing these qualities does not need to be for ourselves. Sometimes my primary motivation to practice has been not for my own sake but for others. I believe that if you practice only for yourself, you are unlikely to sustain your motivation over many years. A significant way to fuel meditation practice is to do it with the wish that it will somehow benefit others and yourself.

We all have long-term and short-term motivations. Experiences of realization may be worthy of long-term goals. Still, in the short term, modest aims may be more beneficial—for example, cultivating small but noticeable improvements in concentration, non-distraction, compassion, or patience can be useful. We can also become aware of small, immediate movements toward letting go and experiencing freedom. There is a beautiful way in which practicing with small, realistic goals allows for a steady maturing into some of the more developed areas of meditation practice.

It's also important to discern whether your aspiration is appropriate given your present situation. If the goals you have set are unrealistic because of time limitations, opportunities, abilities, or disposition, the result will be frustration, a state counterproductive to a practice meant to increase freedom from suffering. While grand aspirations can inspire us—there is no need to be afraid of our heart's deepest wish—it's invaluable to focus on each step along the way realistically. For example, if our body carries a lot of tension, it may be important first to focus on deep relaxation. Or, if our minds are easily distracted, cultivating mental discipline might be needed before hoping for enlightenment.

Understanding Yourself

While motivation is important, does your aspiration match who you are? You might read a book that convinces you that you should do A, B, and C, but you may need something else to suit your life at this time. Or maybe what your teacher is telling you is not a fit. For instance, if we need to focus on our ethics, it may not be appropriate to spend a lot of time on a practice focused on liberation.

Do you know how you learn best? Some people learn best by reading, others by listening, others by watching, and others by doing. Some do best when they have discipline and structure. Others learn best through playfulness, self-direction, or intuitive experimentation. Some people find reading and studying helpful; others may not. Extroverts might find it beneficial to discuss their meditation with friends; introverts may find they work best when they have quiet time for personal reflection. Knowing yourself in these ways makes it more likely you'll find an approach to meditation that suits you. Since it's important not to tailor a meditation practice around personal preferences and attachments, asking a meditation teacher or another meditation practitioner for feedback about your approach to the practice can be helpful.

31

Skillful Evaluation of Meditation Practice, Part 2

Understanding Meditation Instruction

You may be strongly motivated to meditate but need to learn how to do the practice. I meet many meditators who are vague about what they do in meditation beyond relaxing and trying to develop some focus. Some people know the basic instruction but need to learn how to practice with the difficulties that may occur while attempting to follow those instructions. Some people who practice mindfulness meditation may know how to be mindful of their breath or body sensations but need more understanding about how to be mindful of emotions or mental states. In Insight meditation, there is a whole series of instructions for working with the breath, body, emotions, thoughts, and intentions, as well as for walking meditation and mindful speaking. It is important to be familiar with them all.

Do you have a sense of the relationship between meditation practice and your daily life? Hopefully, for Buddhists, our whole life is our practice. Do you know how to live your everyday life so that it supports your meditation? And conversely, do you know how to meditate so that it benefits your daily life? In his book The Practice of the Wild, the poet Gary Snyder wrote:

All of us are apprenticed to the same teacher that the religious institutions originally worked with: reality. Reality Insight says, "Master the 24 hours, do it well, without self-pity." It is as hard to get the children herded into the carpool and down the road to the bus as it is to chant sutras in the Buddha Hall on a cold morning. One move is not better than the other; each can be quite boring, and they both have the virtuous quality of repetition. Repetition and ritual and their good results come in many forms: changing the oil filter, wiping noses, going to meetings, picking up around the house, washing dishes, checking the dipstick. Don't let yourself think these are distracting you from your more serious pursuits. Such a round of chores is not a set of difficulties we hope to escape from so that we may do our practice, which will put us on the path. It is our path.

Another possibility is that you might understand the instructions but may not be sensitive to the unhelpful qualities of mind you bring to practice. The meditation won't unfold well if you strive, expect, hesitate, or make little effort. As a result, the mind never settles into concentration.

Our attitude toward practice is very important. Is there adequate patience, equanimity, kindness, energy, and discipline? Can you find the balance between having a goal in practice and, at the same time, present in a way that is not preoccupied with the goal?

Balance

Is your life balanced enough to support a regular and useful meditation practice? Adding meditation to a life packed with too many activities can be counterproductive. Do you have a healthy balance between work and time off? Is there an appropriate balance between time with others and time alone? Do you get enough exercise so that a good sense of vitality supports your practice? Do you get enough sleep to stay awake during meditation? Some people need sleep more than meditation.

Several factors need to come into balance during meditation itself. There is a balance between faith and wisdom or confidence and understanding. There's also a balance between energy and concentration. Teachings on the factors of awakening stress the importance of balancing the quieting forces of tranquility, concentration, and equanimity with the activating forces of investigation, effort, and joy.

The balance between the body and the mind is also important to attend to. Ideally, meditation practice engages both. It's beneficial in meditation to cultivate a balanced posture that allows for a dynamic interplay of physical relaxation with alertness or uprightness. It's possible to develop a body that is both soft and strong. It's much easier to work with the mind in meditation if the body has been included from the start.

Obstacles

What are your obstacles in meditation practice? Where are the attachments? Where do you get stuck? Are there any regular patterns to the challenges you have in meditation?

One of the important ways to sharpen your meditation practice is to understand the most common difficulties you meet in meditation. Among many challenges meditators encounter are obsessive thinking, desires, aversions, sluggishness, restlessness, psychological or emotional issues, fear of altered states, boredom, complacency, and excessive striving. Attachment to pleasure or resistance to discomfort may also interfere. Getting familiar with which obstacles are most common in your practice can help you become more skillful in working with them.

Unethical or unskillful behavior can also be a significant obstacle to deeper states of meditation. Here's a story that points to this idea:

Some years ago, at an alcohol treatment center in the suburbs of Chicago, staff members reported an intriguing discovery. Many of the counselors lived

*some distance from the facility, commuting daily
via a toll road. Then one day, the state of Illinois
instituted an honor system in the toll collection
booths in the area. No attendant, no barrier gate,
just a basket into which motorists were expected to
toss their coins. Staff at the treatment center made
observations that soon added up to an axiom:
counselors who don't throw their money in, their
patients don't get well. As one counselor phrased it,
"How can you instill honesty in a program if you're
not honest yourself? Honesty is indivisible."*

~From The Spirituality of Imperfection
by Ernest Kurtz and Katherine Ketcham

Another interesting thing to look at is how much self
is involved when you practice. Excessive involvement in
self-judgment, self-criticism, self-image, and self-aggran-
dizement undermines meditation practice. All meditation
practices require the relaxing of self-preoccupation. Just
like it's hard to ride a bike when the body is extremely
stiff, the tensions that arise when we're too concerned
with the self can make it very difficult for the mind to
soften enough to settle into meditation.

Every meditator has challenges. Rather than viewing
obstacles as problems or as unfortunate distractions, it's
more beneficial to patiently and contentedly learn the
skills and Insights that can transform them into stepping

stones along the path of practice. Every meditation tradition has its own approach to working with meditation obstacles. Learn to recognize your own barriers, and then you might ask a meditation teacher to suggest ways of practicing with them.

Insight

An essential aspect of Insight practice is appreciating the Insights that arise. The development of Insight is not just a matter of becoming calm, but also of understanding how your mind works, how your heart works, and what the causes and conditions of suffering and liberation are. As you look more deeply, can you see how you create a sense of self out of all this?

We often take the self for granted. But Buddhist practice shows us that much of what we think of as self is a construct, an activity shaped moment by moment. When you see this creative aspect, you can gain freeing Insight.

We can also have Insight into beautiful states of mind: how compassion works or how to cultivate loving-kindness. Understanding these states helps to cultivate and strengthen them. One purpose of meeting with a teacher is to discuss your understanding and Insights. "This is the understanding I've come to. What do you think of that?"

The most crucial Insight is understanding how clinging works—grasping and clinging in all its gross and subtle forms. All of Buddhism will open up for you if you know the nature of clinging, what you cling to, and how to let go.

Recognizing the Benefits of Practice

Sooner or later, our practice brings benefits. Some-times you have to be patient; sometimes, the benefits are immediate. Ideally, you see how even a single moment of meditation has immediate benefits. At the same time, I hope practitioners understand how meditation can lead them to the possibility of liberation.

Over time, meditation should bring clear benefits such as greater compassion, joy, ease, and self-understanding. Some people discover greater capacities for courage and resolve. Others feel increased appreciation and gratitude. And hopefully, one finds increased experiences of freedom. If you don't experience any of these benefits after a couple years of regular meditation practice, it is important to reevaluate what you're doing. The criteria in this article could point to ways that meditation can be improved. It may be time to discuss your meditation practice with a good teacher. However, I hope that all meditators can become their own teachers. Evaluating our own practice wisely is an important step toward such independence.

32

Practicing in Online Retreats

An innovative opportunity in our modern technological world is online meditation retreats. Rather than traveling to a retreat center, the retreat comes to our homes. While home retreats are not new, in the past they were often solitary, with people practicing alone. In contrast, online retreats provide a clear sense of practicing at home together with others who are also participating from their homes. A community is formed around the online participants who share the same retreat schedule and teachings. Through web-based video conferencing platforms, meditators can see each other meditating, listen to the same teachers, hear the questions and concerns of other retreatants, and engage in group meetings with mentors.

Doing a retreat at home places meditation practice in the location where we live our everyday life. We can bring our mindfulness into ordinary activities, which are often seen as mundane or distracting from our "practice. "Rather than pursuing extraordinary "spiritual experiences" that are apart from everyday life, ordinary tasks like washing dishes, folding laundry, and cooking become "spiritual," — i.e., in Buddhist terms, they become the means to our liberation.

An essential part of home retreats is practicing in such a way that we are in harmony with any housemates, family, or pets with whom we share our homes. Ideally, and most beneficially, this would mean learning to be with others in a way that is in harmony with being on retreat. For example, if conversations are needed, we can discover how to speak in a relaxed, mindful manner that neither disrupts the continuity of the retreat nor disrupts our relationships. If caring for the welfare of others is necessary at home, this caring becomes as much a domain of mindfulness and concentration as sitting in meditation.

Of course, the context for online retreats is very different from practicing at a retreat center. At a center, many of our daily needs are cared for by others. Other retreatants or staff do the shopping, cooking, and cleaning. For a home retreat, practitioners commonly need to do this for themselves. All the necessary domestic tasks can become integrated into the retreat as "work meditations." As such, these jobs can be done as consciously and mindfully as they are on a residential retreat.

Additionally, there is the opportunity to do them as an expression of generosity, care, and love for oneself. "Work meditations" are equally "kind-regard meditations." We can do these tasks as a clear and respectful way of supporting ourselves in retreat. In this way, when we sit down to meditate, we can recognize that we are supporting and caring for ourselves—that we are in a supportive community with ourselves.

Online retreats may require greater personal discipline than residential retreats, where the group momentum provided by in person retreatants help carry one along from one event to another. Practicing at home alone, we may not experience this shared momentum. We may need to evoke dedication and self-discipline to continue meditating through the day. Developing strength and discipline is extremely useful; they will be needed to stay close to the heart's liberation once this is discovered. Online retreats at home certainly have their challenges, not least because some of our greatest attachments may be more manifest at home. Rather than going to a retreat center to escape our everyday preoccupations and attachments, we can face them and find our freedom in the midst of them. For this reason, many people have been surprised at how valuable and transformative practicing at home can be. Rather than having the idea that mindfulness practice and retreat practice are separate from their daily challenges and joys, they discover how to practice right at the center of the challenges and joys.

At the end of a home retreat, we don't have to "return" home. Instead, we have developed new understandings, associations, and routines for practicing at home. For example, making our bed in the morning can become an effective barometer of our inner state. Walking through our home may be associated with walking meditation, supporting greater mindfulness throughout the day. Inspired by the greater embodied mindfulness we experienced in the kitchen during the online retreat, we may begin to cook in everyday life with fewer distracting thoughts.

One dictionary definition of retreat is "a period of seclusion for the purposes of prayer and meditation." With this meaning, the word is closely related to the concept of sanctuary—i.e., a place where the sacred is found. Home retreats can teach us how to see our home as a sanctuary in ordinary life. Meditation retreats are not a withdrawal from the "real world"; they are a withdrawal from the distractions, preoccupations, and fantasies that keep us from the "real world." Being on retreat entails stepping back from distraction and delusion in order to be with the world in a new way—experiencing our life clearly, calmly, and without the overlays of our mental projections. It's a time to discover the sanctuary of a liberated heart and to carry this sanctuary into all areas of our life. In this sense, meditation retreats become an entry into the world, not retreating from the world. Both symbolically and in actuality, participating at home in an online retreat represents waking up to the "real world" more than leaving home for a retreat somewhere else.

Online retreats have opened up many new opportunities and made it possible for more people to attend retreats and attend more often. These retreats can include more people than a retreat center can accommodate, and they make participation possible for those who can't travel or leave home. People from all over the world can participate, and together create a global community of practitioners. These retreats have also made it possible to experiment with various new ways to participate. Some people seclude themselves at home to meditate much of the time. Others continue with their usual work while dipping into the retreat through the day, perhaps listening to the teachings as much as they meditate.

The closing of retreat centers during the pandemic made online retreats an option. We learned there are many benefits that come with holding retreats in this way. Online retreats are here to stay. Those participating in these retreats during the first year of our new online retreat era are the pioneers of an exciting expansion of the practice. We are laying down the foundation for people to benefit from online retreats for years to come.

33

Self Retreats

Having gone to the wilderness,
a foot of a tree, or an empty building,
a practitioner sits down
with legs crossed and body erect.
Establishing awareness to the forefront,
always attentive,
one breathes in with awareness
and breathes out with awareness.

~The Buddha (Anapanasati Sutta)

After participating in several teacher-led Insight meditation retreats, whether in person or online, the next step could be a self-retreat, which provides valuable opportunities and challenges for continuing to develop Dharma practice. Self-retreats require greater discipline and resolve than are usually needed at group retreats. Because of this, these retreats can awaken greater confidence in the practice and our ability to do it.

Some people discover they benefit from the radical simplicity of well-prepared self-retreats. Meditating away from everyday responsibilities and concerns can create a sanctuary-like place and time to connect with the Dharma and ourselves. It can be a time to allow unrecognized agitation and preoccupations to be known and fade away. The minimalism of a self-retreat can allow for greater letting go, which, in turn, may bring us close to our heart's deepest values, intentions, and wisdom.

Self-retreats are not for escaping everyday life. They are opportunities to touch something profoundly important about life and oneself that is easily drowned out by daily activities and social interactions. While group retreats can be very supportive and create a unique and wonderful sense of community, self-retreats provide different lessons and discoveries that can appear when we meditate alone, apart from other meditators.

Historically—down through the centuries—self-retreats have been the predominant way to engage in extended periods of meditation, sometimes for days, weeks, months, or longer. In ancient India, Buddhists lived in the forest and other natural settings while on retreat. Rather than having other meditators for support, they had the natural world.

When we begin doing self-retreats, it's helpful to start with one or two days. When the rhythm of practice on self-retreat becomes familiar enough, we can set aside a longer period. It is best not to do a self-retreat longer than your most extended teacher-led retreat; this ensures you will already have familiarity with the rhythm of the retreat from beginning to end.

Self-retreats can be done at home if one has enough privacy. They can also be done in a secluded location where there are no reminders of home and work. In either case, the place should be well-stocked with all that is needed, or else arrange deliveries ahead of time, so there is no need to go shopping during the retreat. Meals can be pre-cooked or simple to make.

Using or adapting the schedule from a teacher-led retreat can create a useful structure and rhythm for a self-retreat. It might be supportive to follow a fixed schedule closely, especially the first few times you practice in this way. Using a schedule can free up a lot of energy that otherwise would go toward deciding what to do next and for how long.

For well-experienced retreatants who have done at least six week-long retreats and several self-retreats, it can be valuable to do a self-retreat with no schedule and no clock. Live a simple life where you do nothing extra that is not part of the retreat. Don't have a plan for when you will meditate, eat, sleep, etc. Do each when you feel it supports your overall retreat. If it doesn't feel right to do the usual retreat activities, sit by a window looking at nothing until you feel the call to continue with them. Having a schedule-free retreat allows you to be guided by how your practice unfolds.

For people new to self-retreats, it can be helpful to have daily Dharma teachings. These could be recorded talks, for example, from a teacher-led retreat, or short Dharma readings. You might read one- or two-page Dharma passages a few times throughout the day. At some point, people with quite a bit of experience with self-retreats might try omitting Dharma teachings altogether. The absence of teachings can help maintain a radical simplicity in which everything is processed through meditation and the meditative life of the retreat. The practice itself provides plenty of teachings.

It's most supportive of a self-retreat to have no connection to email, social media, or the web. Such contact can very quickly challenge whatever calm and clarity we've developed. But if it's truly needed, it's important to commit to the bare minimum. If you plan to listen to recorded Dharma talks, download them before the retreat, on a device that won't tempt you to reconnect to the digital world.

One of the significant benefits of a self-retreat is the opportunity for continuity of practice throughout the day. If the daily logistics for the retreat are simple, being alone lessens the chances for an interruption in mindfulness when not meditating. A self-retreat is a time when the whole day can be a meditation, a Dharma life.

Loneliness is one of the potential challenges of a self-retreat. If it is particularly strong, it might not be the right time for a self-retreat. When it is not too strong, loneliness is invaluable to investigate with mindfulness. Being lonely is different than being alone. Loneliness stems from having particular thoughts, reactions, and desires. Seeing these clearly and learning to be patient with them is training in the valuable life skill of patience. Understanding how loneliness might be connected to significant unresolved emotions can show you where to direct your compassion and mindfulness. When loneliness abates or disappears, you might discover a deeper connection to yourself; you can become your own best friend. Seeing loneliness through to the other side can be incredibly freeing. Social relationships after the retreat can benefit from this freedom. Occasions for being alone may be more welcoming and beneficial after shedding the tendency to be lonely.

Because we are able to design self-retreats for ourselves, it's helpful to include what supports us to practice well. This support may or may not include exercise. Some form of walking or movement throughout the day is important for maintaining balance in meditation. We can choose wake-up and sleep times that work for our biorhythms. We can personalize how gradually we enter and leave the heart of the retreat. Some people benefit from a slow return to daily life.

For longer self-retreats, it could be useful to have some phone contact with an Insight teacher. This could be on an as-needed basis or one time during a weeklong retreat and once a week for longer retreats.

Meditation self-retreats can be powerful and effective ways of deepening one's Buddhist practice. They are so valuable that it is best to approach them with respect and humility. Engage in the retreat to see what the practice brings, letting go of expectations and goals for specific outcomes. Practice sincerely and trust the value of practicing with whatever comes.

34

Sharing the Benefits of Retreat Practice

*We practice within a wheel of giving and
  receiving.*
*May we keep this Dharma wheel turning to
  benefit all beings.*
*With whatever benefits we receive from prac-
  tice, may these serve us to benefit others.*
*With whatever benefits we receive from others,
  may these inspire us to benefit ourselves.*
*May we give so we can receive, receive so we can
  give.*
*May we share our goodness to others. and
  receive the goodness of others.*
*May we share our goodness with ourselves and
  receive our own goodness.*
*May we be the still point in the center of the
  wheel,*
*Free from the turning, free to support the turn-
  ing, always allowing giving and receiving to
  roll on peacefully.*

Everything is Practice

APPENDIX

Insight Retreat Center
Mission & Vision

The Mission

IRC is dedicated to offering silent Insight Meditation retreats. We do this residentially at our Santa Cruz retreat center and online via videoconferencing. We emphasize the practice of Buddhist ideals – mindfulness, ethics, compassion, loving-kindness, and liberation. Based on a 2500-year-old Buddhist teaching, this practice helps us to see more deeply and clearly into our lives. With Insight, we develop ways of living more peacefully, compassionately, and wisely.

Generosity is a cornerstone of IRC. Liberation practices develop most beautifully and effectively when we offer the Dharma freely. There is no cost for attending our retreats; they're offered freely to those who are sincerely interested in participating in this kind of practice. All our expenses, including those needed to care for our 3.8-acre facility, are covered by voluntary, non-obligatory donations. These come from those participating in our retreats and from our community of supporters and volunteers.

Our center is run entirely through the generosity of our many volunteers. These include our resident volunteers, who take care of much of the day-to-day operations of our center when retreats are not being held. During retreats, the daily operations, such as cooking, cleaning, and general management, are done by the retreatants as part of their retreat practice. In addition, our large team of non-residential volunteers cares for IRC's administration, finances, and technology throughout the year.

We are a "community-based retreat center" entirely sustained by the broad community of practitioners and supporters inspired by the retreat practice, teachings, and values found at the center. The heart of IRC—fueling IRC—is this community's goodwill, goodness, and generosity, for which we are enormously grateful.

Vision for IRC

While continuing to hold residential retreats is a significant part of our ongoing vision for IRC, we now realize the great benefit of online retreats. During the first eighteen months of the pandemic when holding in-person retreats wasn't possible, online retreats became our sole offering, and the benefits became apparent. Now, many people who are unable to attend our residential retreats can participate in retreat practice online. Many practitioners who have previously participated in residential retreats have found that practicing from home during online retreats has brought the practice into their daily lives in new and significant ways. We, therefore, have a vision of continuing to develop our online retreat offerings.

With our great desire to alleviate suffering in our world and awaken greater peace, wisdom, compassion, and goodwill in many people's hearts, we aspire to meet the growing interest in Insight meditation, and Insight meditation retreats. For this purpose, one of our aims is to train more Insight Meditation teachers. We also aim to find more ways to bring the Dharma to a greater range of people and communities.

We dream of a second residential Insight retreat center that would allow us to expand the types of retreats and training we can offer. Part of this dream, however, is to do so in a way that reflects the ease that Insight practice fosters and develops. So instead of striving to grow and expand, we will be enthusiastically available when inspiration, support, and conditions come together to make such an expansion possible. It will then be our task to express our spiritual practice in creating and running a second center.

The Practice of a Service Leader

At the Insight Retreat Center, the practice of serving as a service leader is an opportunity to manifest the Dharma—that is, to express the values, Insights, and freedoms that come with the practice as integral aspects of ourselves. As such, the service offered is equally to ourselves, our fellow Service Leaders, the participants of a retreat, and any person or being who happens to wander onto the IRC property.

From the widest perspective, to engage in "Dharma service" is to serve out of care for the welfare of all beings. On a retreat, service leaders care for the well-being of all participants through the tasks appropriate for the particular role they hold for a retreat. Cooks serve through the food they make, through their care for the retreatants who work in the kitchen, and in the Dharma practice they bring to their role and work. Managers serve through all their interactions with retreatants, and through attending to the practical, logistical, and health needs of participants and the retreat as a whole. Importantly both cooks and managers serve through the way they model the Dharma in their practice during the retreat.

Because service leaders manifest the Dharma through their actions, they should be mature enough in practice to have discovered the Dharma in themselves. They know that ethical integrity, kindness and compassion, generosity, wise speech, and non-clinging are personal qualities with which they wish to serve. Service Leaders do not need to be told that these qualities are the basis of a Dharma life; they know them to be the basis for how they want to live. Sometimes service work is done to express motivations arising out of Dharma practice. Other times, people engage in service work as a practice—occasionally difficult— in which they discover how to work and interact with others to be attuned to these wholesome traits. The sincere effort to do this is a service leader's gift, even if the effort proves to be difficult.

Serving as Cooks

Cooking in a Dharma center is a uniquely multidimensional opportunity to practice. More aspects of ourselves and life can be encountered in the kitchen than in the meditation hall. For this reason, we call kitchen practice "kitchen training" to better represent the many aspects of ourselves that are involved.

Kitchen training is interactive in that cooks are constantly in a relationship with something or someone. They work with the food to cook nutritious dishes for the bodies and hearts of fellow retreatants. They are touching, holding, and caring for kitchen implements as extensions of themselves. They are collaborating with the other cooks as a mutually supportive team. They are mindful and caring toward fellow retreatants doing work meditation in the kitchen. And in doing work that directly impacts everyone on a retreat, their work is a conduit for their respect and love of others.

As their kitchen work puts them at the nexus of many relationships, the cooks' mindfulness and intention have many, often simultaneous facets. In navigating this rich field of relationships, four primary Dharma tasks lay at the foundation of a cook's practice.

The first task of a cook is to avoid being distracted from their work. Simple and direct attention to the matter at hand is the basis for the Dharma of cooking. It creates the opening for the Dharma to appear in the midst of the kitchen activity.

The second task is to let go of any conceit, anxiety, and rumination that might interfere with the work. While these may occur, a wise cook gives them no authority or priority. To identify with conceit, anxiety, and rumination is to block a direct connection to the practice and the

Dharma. And it also limits the joy of cooking.

The third task is to cook with love. This is done through feelings of care, kindness, compassion, generosity, respect, and appreciation for everyone on the retreat. It is enough that the cook has rudimentary seeds for love, even if it is only the wish to love. Trusting and valuing these seeds while cooking is a way for them to germinate and grow.

The fourth task is to work in beauty. Dharma beauty combines goodness, virtuousness, big-heartedness, generosity, happiness, and gratitude. Beauty can appear when there is clarity and ease in one's awareness of the present moment. When awareness is perceived as beautiful, there may be a subjective sense that everything one sees, touches, smells, and hears in the kitchen is permeated with this beauty, even things that may be, in conventional ways, not beautiful. Keeping their workspace reasonably clean, orderly, and beautiful supports the possibility of working in Dharma beauty. Presenting a meal with some attention to the beauty of the presentation can support the Dharma beauty of the retreatants.

The idea of "working in beauty" includes practicing with equanimity, ease, and even delight when, after the cooks' best efforts, a meal is not ready on time, or the main dish is burned. They do not take cooking accidents as personal mistakes. Rather than being alarmed, upset, or discouraged, cooks simply take stock of the situation and devote themselves to the next thing that needs to happen. In this way, the cooks become teachers of the retreat, demonstrating non-clinging and devotion, without seeing anything as a problem, doing what is needed wholeheartedly and without reservation, and hopefully experiencing the joy of service.

The Insight Retreat Center has two hearts; one is the meditation hall, and the second is the kitchen. These two hearts join at the start of each meal when retreatants come down from the meditation hall, and cooks come out of the kitchen and bow to each other. That bow represents the coming together of Dharma practice and Dharma service.

Serving as a Manager

The work of IRC managers is conveyed in the Pali word for "manage"—i.e., *upatthahati*. The Pali-English dictionary defines this as "to stand near or at hand, to wait on, attend on, serve, minister, to care for, look after, nurse." In this sense, the managers are the two people who stand at the center of the retreat, ready to offer whatever service is needed so the retreat can operate smoothly and retreatants have favorable conditions to practice.

First and foremost, managers support everyone at the retreat. Managers do their best to practice unconditional appreciation of all retreatants. This appreciation includes assuming every person on the retreat is practicing the best they can. In this way, retreatants view managers as supportive throughout the retreat. To be available during their shift, managers should do their sitting and walking meditation in places where they are easily found—e.g., in the meditation hall and the community room. Managers are also understated cheerleaders, offering occasional, simple expressions of appreciation to those they have reason to speak with.

Ideally, managers have a grandparent's love for each retreatant. This equanimous care is never alarmed but always ready to offer kindness and support. Care arises from a manager's own practice, especially letting go of all that interferes with having a tender, caring heart in meetings with others. By letting go during the regular meditations and in interactions with retreatants, a manager's goodwill develops in the direction of becoming natural and simple, and not complicated by any attempt at forced or artificial kindness.

To be a manager is to practice having the view that everything that happens is equally an opportunity for practice. It is as valuable to meditate as it is to reply to a retreatant's note, to look for cough drops, to drive someone to urgent care, or to figure out how to adjust the lights in the meditation hall. Helping a retreatant clean up food and a broken plate from the dining room floor is as much the manager's practice of compassionate care as sitting with someone for whom the manager relayed a message of a death in the family.

While managing, managers exemplify being free of self-focused practice. Ideas of "my practice," "my valued state of mind," "my personal time," or "my preferences" are put aside. Managers are not "practicing for themselves" in a self-centered way; they are simply practicing responding appropriately to whatever the situation needs, whether this is inside or outside of themselves. Managers do not need to bother themselves with thoughts that they are "good managers" or "poor managers." Instead, managers practice meeting each situation the best they can without self-preoccupation or self-identity.

There may be times when a manager has to let a retreatant know that what they are doing doesn't fit with the practice of IRC. In doing so, managers should be careful to avoid viewing the retreatant as wrong. They can simply explain that at IRC we do things differently. When strong boundary setting is needed or when someone needs to be asked to leave, the art of managing entails being kind while making clear that the behavior at issue isn't suitable for retreats at IRC; it's the retreatant's choice either to change or—if unwilling or unable to do so—to leave. Even in such conversations, rare as they are, the manager should continue to attempt to be a supporter of the retreatant.

The teachers of a retreat are important supports for managers. When managers are uncertain how to bring their practice to any challenging aspect of their work, they can consult with a teacher.

Like the teachers, the managers are the most visible people at the retreat who represent the values and practices at IRC. This makes managing an excellent opportunity to learn and model "to care and not to care," to be compassionate and not attached.

The Role of IRC Teachers

Together with everyone else on the retreat, teachers are also practitioners on the retreat. Just as cooks practice in cooking, managers in managing, dishwashers in dishwashing, and veggie choppers in chopping, so teachers practice in teaching. As with all these activities, teaching is approached as a way to grow in love, freedom, and awakening.

Teachers have unique roles. To the degree that "the medium is the message," how a teacher practices on retreat is as important as what they teach. The teacher's confidence and dedication to the Dharma can be a significant support for everyone on the retreat. This is conveyed through what they say and, perhaps more powerfully, through how teachers practice on the retreat.

Every participant has a role in supporting the retreat. Part of the teachers' role is to carry the responsibility for the retreat as a whole. If unexpected issues arise that others are unsure how to handle, it is the teachers' responsibility to investigate and make decisions if necessary. This means they may need to respond to issues not usually considered within the scope of a Dharma teacher's role. For example, while a facilities caretaker is available for each retreat, a teacher may have to participate in decisions and coordination if urgent facility issues arise. While retreat managers will do their best to support the retreatants, if major issues arise, teachers should be closely involved.

The role of the teacher includes guidance and teachings that support the all-volunteer, community–led approach of IRC retreats. The teachers' emphasis is on the Dharma of goodwill, generosity, and gratitude as well as helping everyone feel welcome. All teachers have an important role in emphasizing that everyone is creating the retreat together and that everyone is sharing in the practice and the care for the retreat.

Code of Ethics for IMC/IRC Teachers

This document applies to all people who function in the following roles at IRC, IMC or in any IMC-related events, programs, or offerings: teachers, including senior students serving in a teaching role, guest teachers, mentors, chaplains, and ministers.

The foundation of spiritual life rests upon our mindful and caring relationship to the life around us. In keeping with this understanding and for the long-¬term benefit of all, we agree to uphold the five lay training precepts.

In this Code of Ethics, we explicitly expand the scope of the five precepts to make them appropriate to our specific cultural setting.

1) We undertake the precept of refraining from harming living beings.

We acknowledge the interconnection of all beings and maintain a reverence for all life. We will refrain from all forms of violence. We will develop our understanding of non-harming. We seek to help students understand the implications of this precept in ways that support their practice.

2) We undertake the precept of refraining from taking that which is not offered.

We will not take what belongs to others unless it is

freely given. We will bring consciousness to the use of all of the earth's resources in a respectful and ecologically sensitive way. We will be honest in dealing with money and not misappropriate money committed to Dharma projects. We will offer teachings and Dharma support freely.

3) We undertake the precept of refraining from sexual misconduct.

We will avoid creating harm through sexual conduct and will refrain from all forms of sexual exploitation. In particular, we will not use our teaching role to pursue or encourage a sexual relationship with a student; nor will we accept or accede to sexual interest or advances from a student. In order to nurture an atmosphere of safety, we will model and encourage non-sexualized communications and behavior.

With respect to relationships between a teacher and a student, we will abide by the following agreements:

a. Teachers will refrain from engaging in sexual activity with students without exception, including refraining from any speech or action on the part of the teacher indicating or implying sexual interest in a student.

b. Teachers will remain mindful of the ways students and teachers alike can engage in transference and/or projection of feelings, including sexual feelings, onto the student-teacher relationship. When a teacher recognizes this is occurring, the teacher will consult with wise peers, their guiding teacher, and possibly another professional in order to protect and maintain the safety and integrity of the student-teacher relationship.

c. If mutual consensual interest in a sexual relationship occurs between someone in a teaching role and someone in a student role, then the teacher-student relationship must definitively end before a sexual relationship begins. Once the student and teacher mutually agree that their student-teacher relationship has ended, there will follow an extended period of limited contact between the two. The details of this limited contact are to be established with the guidance of the EAR Council and the guiding teacher(s) at IMC (or their designee). A typical time frame for this limited contact period will likely range from 3-12 months but will vary. The predetermined period of limited contact must elapse before any sexual relationship is entered into.

4) We undertake the precept of refraining from false and harmful speech.

We will speak what is true and useful and refrain from harsh speech, divisive speech, and disparaging speech. In addition, we aspire to speak in ways that are increasingly inclusive and respectful of all people. We will cultivate

conscious and clear communication and the quality of loving-kindness as the basis of our speech in order to support
the development of harmony among students in the sangha. Teachers will support sangha members to speak in
ways that are sensitive to all beings and that promote a
community where people feel free to speak what they
believe is true. Teachers will preserve the privacy of students and not share identifying details of students' practice
histories or stories without their consent.

5) We undertake the precept of refraining from intoxicants that cause heedlessness or loss of awareness.

We will not abuse intoxicants and we will refrain from
all use of intoxicants in the presence of students. If any
teacher has a drug or alcohol addiction problem, the
Guiding Teachers and the IMC Board of Directors commit to addressing the situation. In order to facilitate a supportive environment for all students adhering to this precept, teachers will endeavor to keep IMC-related events,
programs, and gatherings free of intoxicants.

Ethics and Reconciliation Council

The EAR Council

The Ethics and Reconciliation (EAR) Council is a group of three to five IMC practitioners, respected for their integrity, who are available to any community member requesting help in dealing with ethical concerns, conflicts, and grievances within the IMC community, including conflicts with teachers. The IMC Board appoints council members to three-year terms, following the same procedure for the election of board members.

Background

Ethical concerns and conflict will inevitably arise within the IMC community. The health of our community is not measured by the presence or absence of conflict but by our willingness to find an effective, responsible, and compassionate resolution of interpersonal tensions when they arise. The commitment to attend to and learn from conflict is a clear application of Buddhist practice in our daily lives. With this intention, practice with conflict can become a deeply transformative vehicle for our lives.

Buddhist ethics and conflict-resolution go beyond right or wrong, blame or guilt, winning or losing, offenders or victims. Rather, they are based on compassionately addressing the suffering of all concerned. Hurt, fear, and anger are taken seriously through forums where all parties may speak honestly, safely, and completely about their own direct experiences and feelings. In seeking resolution, Buddhist practice values dialogue over silence, reconciliation over estrangement, forgiveness over resentment, taking responsibility for harm caused by one's actions over assigning blame, and making amends over punishment. Because the process of reaching such resolution is often difficult, IMC's Ethics and Reconciliation Council offers support and guidance.

The Insight Meditation Center is committed to cultivating an inclusive and ethically sensitive practice environment. The creation of the EAR Council is an expression of our commitment to build supportive structures for the Sangha around ethical concerns that arise within our community as well as conflict resolution. Periodically it is appropriate to review and revise IMC's Ethics and Reconciliation Council procedures and its Teachers' Code of Ethics. Both documents were reviewed and revised in 2019.

PRIMARY PROCEDURE:
Provide Consultation and/or Support Reconciliation
Confidential Consultation

Any sangha member may approach any EAR Council member for consultation. The primary role of EAR Council members is to provide confidential consultation to anyone with concerns about ethical issues or conflicts within the IMC/IRC community. When appropriate the preference of the Council is to seek reconciliation between all parties in dispute. When an EAR Council member is approached by a sangha member with a concern, the EAR Council member will notify the other members of the Council, and the Council will determine how it can best be of service to the parties concerned and the sangha as a whole. Some of the ways the Council may respond include:

a. as confidential sounding boards for a sangha member's (or sangha members') concerns;

b. as a source of guidance for deeper personal reflection and practice around an ethical issue or a conflict that has arisen;

c. as a source of advice on how best to resolve a particular conflict that has arisen with another sangha member or teacher;

d. to facilitate skillful discussion and reconciliation between parties in conflict or in other ways bring conflict to a satisfactory resolution; and/or

e. for matters that require immediate action to protect the safety of IMC and community members, the EAR Council member in consultation with other EAR Council members and Board Executive Committee will contact the relevant legal or health authorities.

SECONDARY PROCEDURE:

Grievance Process

On the rare occasion that a more formal process is necessary, and following the above primary sequence of steps, the following grievance procedure is available.

1) Bringing a Concern

A formal grievance procedure is initiated by submitting a letter of request to the Council that includes:

- A statement that a formal grievance procedure is requested.
- The name of the person(s) or party whose behavior or policy the complaint involves.
- A detailed written description of the alleged behavior.
- A history of attempt(s), if any, to resolve the complaint through other means, including the primary reconciliation procedures listed above.
- A general statement about the resolution desired.

2) Accepting the Concern

The EAR Council will first determine whether the issue is directly related to the sangha and to members of the sangha and the relationships therein. Once it has been determined if the concerns expressed fall within the scope of the EAR Council's responsibilities, the EAR Council will convey its decision to the parties involved as promptly as possible. As part of this notification, the Council will state its understanding of the issue under inquiry in writing and will distribute this document and a copy of the original letter of request to the party named in the complaint. If the Council does not accept a request, it will communicate its reasons for doing so in writing to the initiating party and may recommend further mediation or another course of action. In some cases, outside mediation may be recommended.

3) Forming a Grievance Committee

When a complaint is accepted, one member of the EAR Council will convene and facilitate a Grievance Committee to investigate, issue findings, and render a decision on the complaint. The facilitator will be engaged in discussions and other activities but they will not participate in Committee voting.

The Grievance Committee will be made up of the facilitator and three people selected from past and present IMC Board members, IMC Chaplaincy Council members, and IMC Dharma Leaders. Each party to the grievance will be given an opportunity to request one person for the Grievance Committee from the aforementioned groups.

4) Investigating the Concern

The facilitator will schedule a closed meeting where all parties are given a chance to present their understanding of the issue under investigation. The Grievance Committee may question parties, gather additional information, or schedule additional meetings. If desired, the parties may each bring a supporting companion to such a meeting.

All parties will have an opportunity to respond to all information—oral, written, or other—gathered by the Committee.

The proceedings and all pertinent documents, including any notes taken by Grievance Committee members, will be held confidentially, unless a court requires disclosure.

During the time of investigation, review, and decision-making, an EAR Council member who is not functioning as the Facilitator or serving on the Grievance Committee may function as a source of support for those involved in the conflict at the request of either party.

5) Committee Findings and Recommended Actions

When the Grievance Committee members are satisfied that they are adequately informed, they will review and discuss the grievance among themselves. At its discretion, the Committee may seek non--binding advice from any other source who agrees to hold the matters discussed in confidence. The Committee will endeavor to reach its decision by consensus and present a unanimous finding. If unanimity cannot be reached, committee members will vote. Within two weeks of a decision(s), the Council will email all parties with the result of its deliberations. For matters involving grievances and conflict that could impact IMC and its community in significant ways (such as issues that could lead to the suspension or other sanction of an IMC teacher or that could involve a legal proceeding) the EAR Council will provide its written findings and recommendations to the IMC Board of Directors to determine the best next steps.

Acknowledgements

This book would not have been possible without my teachers and fellow retreatants who supported me in my retreats. I am profoundly grateful to them and how their practice was transmitted as a gift.

This book would also not have been possible without the many practitioners who have attended retreats I have taught. Their practice inspired me. Their questions, practice discussions, and wisdom taught me much more about retreat practice than I learned on my own retreats.

I offer my deep thanks to the many people who have supported me in the writing and editing that also made the book possible, including Carol Ghiglieri, Diana Clark, Ines Freedman, Shelley Gault, and Toren Fronsdal. I thank Elena Silverman for her care and generosity in designing and layout out the book for printing.

About the Author

Gil Fronsdal is the founding teacher of the Insight Meditation Center in Redwood City, California and the Insight Retreat Center in Santa Cruz, California. He has been engaged in the practice, study, and teaching of Buddhism for fifty years.

Gil recorded talks related to mindfulness, meditation, and Buddhist practice are available at Audiodharma.org.

Gil spent time as a Buddhist monk in monasteries in the U.S., Japan, Thailand, and Myanmar. He has a Ph.D. in Buddhist Studies.

His books on Buddhist practice are:
- *The Issue at Hand; Essays on Buddhist Mindfulness Practice*
- *Unhindered: Tales of the Buddhist Path*
- *The Monastery Within: A Mindful Path Through the Five Hindrances*
- *Steps to Liberation: The Buddha's Eightfold Path*

His translations of early Buddhist teachers are:
- *The Dhammapada: A Translation of a Buddhist Classic*
- *The Buddha before Buddhism: Wisdom from the Early Teachings*

Made in the USA
Middletown, DE
10 July 2024

57158465R00124